TAKE HEED THAT YE

Be Not Deceived

First printing: January 1992
Revised and enlarged: July 1992
Revised and enlarged: May 1994
Revised and enlarged: August 1995

RICHARD I. WINWOOD

And [Jesus] said,

Take heed

that ye be not

deceived.

Luke 21:8

The Articles of Faith

1   We believe in God, the Eternal Father, and in His Son, Jesus Christ, and in the Holy Ghost.

2   We believe that men will be punished for their own sins, and not for Adam's transgression.

3   We believe that through the Atonement of Christ, all mankind may be saved, by obedience to the laws and ordinances of the Gospel.

4   We believe that the first principles and ordinances of the Gospel are: first, Faith in the Lord Jesus Christ; second, Repentance; third, Baptism by immersion for the remission of sins; fourth, Laying on of hands for the gift of the Holy Ghost.

5   We believe that a man must be called of God, by prophecy, and by the laying on of hands by those who are in authority, to preach the Gospel and administer in the ordinances thereof.

6   We believe in the same organization that existed in the Primitive Church, namely, apostles, prophets, pastors, teachers, evangelists, and so forth.

7   We believe in the gift of tongues, prophecy, revelation, visions, healing, interpretation of tongues, and so forth.

8   We believe the Bible to be the word of God as far as it is translated correctly; we also believe the Book of Mormon to be the word of God.

9   We believe all that God has revealed, all that He does now reveal, and we believe that He will yet

reveal many great and important things pertaining to the Kingdom of God.

10 We believe in the literal gathering of Israel and in the restoration of the Ten Tribes; that Zion (the New Jerusalem) will be built upon the American continent; that Christ will reign personally upon the earth; and, that the earth will be renewed and receive its paradisiacal glory.

11 We claim the privilege of worshiping Almighty God according to the dictates of our own conscience, and allow all men the same privilege, let them worship how, where, or what they may.

12 We believe in being subject to kings, presidents, rulers, and magistrates, in obeying, honoring, and sustaining the law.

13 We believe in being honest, true, chaste, benevolent, virtuous, and in doing good to all men; indeed, we may say that we follow the admonition of Paul—We believe all things, we hope all things, we have endured many things, and hope to be able to endure all things. If there is anything virtuous, lovely, or of good report or praiseworthy, we seek after these things.

Contents

Acknowledgments

This is the fourth revision and printing of this little book. I've enjoyed researching and writing it, and particularly having the help of many talented and giving people along the way. Each has made my simple expressions look and sound better. As usual, there are always vital few—those whose contributions are truly above the call. I will always be indebted to Spencer Sloane and Matthew Thompson. These two elders worked with me on the original manuscript. Without their insight and hard work, this project would never have gotten off the ground.

Many faithful and honest people have involved themselves in defending and clarifying Mormon doctrine and in enlightening those who have been infected by enemies of the Lord's work. Chief among these faithful are my friends Robert and Rosemary Brown. At great personal sacrifice they have given of themselves to establish truth and expose falsehoods. I know their hearts. They are heroes to me.

Others whom I must mention with deep appreciation are Jim Mills, Peter and Sara Cyngot, Dan Peterson, and Brent Hall. Extra special thanks to Jessica Taylor at FARMS. Jessica is a wizard of research and detail. Working with her is a delight.

In a strange way, I am grateful to opponents of the Church who have argued their philosophies

with me. They have given me a deeper understanding of how Satan works to blind the minds of
men. As I ponder the tactics of those who opposed
the Savior in His earthly ministry, I see shadows in
their modern-day counterparts.

List of Abbreviations

The following is a list of abbreviations used
throughout this work. Complete bibliographic references are provided in the Endnotes or the
Suggested Reading List the end of the book.

AP	Aprocrypha
BM	The Book of Mormon
D&C	The Doctrine and Covenants
JSH	Joseph Smith—History (in PGP)
LDS Church	The Church of Jesus Christ of Latter-day Saints
NT	New Testament
OT	Old Testament
PGP	The Pearl of Great Price

Abbreviations for books of the Bible are traditional
abbreviations, according to the King James Version
of the Bible.

Introduction

I first became aware of The Church of Jesus Christ of Latter-day Saints (the LDS, or Mormon, Church) when I was about twenty-five years old. I was happily married at the time and the father of two young children. My wife and I both had religious upbringing in Protestant churches, and we believed and lived basic Christian principles. But we were attending no church services at the time. In fact, we had given up on churches in general. From our perspective, religious leaders seemed more interested in financial and social issues than in religious ones. Even within our respective church organizations, little agreement on important issues could be found. Moreover, no religious organization known to us was able to answer our simplest questions about life, death, heaven, and so on. Consequently, we became irreligious and very skeptical of those preaching religion. We simply decided to live good lives devoid of any church affiliation.

During this time I was given a copy of the Book of Mormon by a loved one. I ignored the book for many months. When I finally began to read it, my purpose was to learn enough about it to show my dear friend where she had been deceived. What happened then completely changed my life. My interest in demonstrating how the Book of Mormon deceived was replaced by an intense interest in the doctrines it taught clearly and understandably. As I read I began to find answers to my own questions of life. I was impressed by the noble story of the boy prophet, Joseph Smith, who translated the Book of Mormon from golden plates given him by an angel (see pages 14–17 for a short version of this story). His honesty and unpretentious nature impressed me. When I read his history and testimony in the Pearl of Great Price (another book of scripture), I was struck with the forthrightness of his simple but beautiful testimonial statement:

> I had actually seen a light, and in the midst of that light I saw two Personages, and they did in reality speak to me; and though I was hated and persecuted for saying that I had seen a vision, yet it was true; and while they were persecuting me, reviling me, and speaking all manner of evil against me falsely for so saying, I was led to say in my heart: Why persecute me for telling the truth? I have actually seen a vision; and who am I that I can withstand God, or why does the world think to make me deny what I have actually seen? For I had seen a vision; I knew it, and I knew that God knew it, and I could not deny it. (JSH 1:25)

I pondered the situation that the boy Joseph was in when he went to the Sacred Grove to pray and received this First Vision. I then realized that I was in much the same position. I was confused about why there were so many churches. I wondered at the diversity of Christian doctrine and religious practice—it was a mass of confusion to me. Would God be the author of such chaos? Could I enlighten myself by speaking to any religious leader I knew? No, the confusion could only be cleared up by gaining wisdom and truth from on high. James 1:5 held the obvious and completely unique way to know the truth.

As I read of Joseph Smith's experiences and pondered his motives, I was given to know by "the still small voice" (BM, 1 Nephi 17:45), i.e., the Holy Ghost, that he was telling the truth, that his experiences were real. It was a marvelous and completely unexpected affirmation. That simple witness was the beginning of a journey that would change my life forever. The experience is a treasure for my heart.

Later, after my wife and I read more in the Book of Mormon, the Holy Bible, and other inspired scripture and received the missionary discussions, we were impressed to enter the waters of baptism and become members of Christ's true church and to live our lives according to the principles of the restored gospel of Jesus Christ. That event took place on 21 February 1971 in Portland, Oregon.

As new members of the Church, we had to grow in understanding of our new faith. We were given opportunities to serve our "brothers and sisters" in various capacities. We came to love the Church as much as we loved the gospel.

However, almost immediately upon joining the Church, I became aware of a movement outside the Church to discredit the Prophet Joseph Smith, the Book of Mormon, and the Church organization and doctrine. This disturbed me a great deal. I had never had my faith attacked before, nor had I had something sacred to me belittled and scorned by others. Once, a well-meaning friend shared a book with me entitled *Who Really Wrote the Book of Mormon?*[1] I read it with interest. It appeared to be well researched and well documented. It proclaimed that the Book of Mormon was a fake and that Joseph Smith was a liar. These were heavy words to me. They struck me to the center. Had I been deceived? Had my encounters with the Spirit been simply my overactive emotion? I was troubled and shaken. I wanted answers. After some extensive research, I found the answers I was looking for.

I discovered that the book my friend gave me was filled with errors and statements of half-truth. The authors openly lied about historical facts. They used scriptures as Satan would—ignoring or distorting the true meaning. Quotes and references were made to sources that appeared, on the surface, to be valid but proved to be spurious and reprehensible. The book was a cover-to-cover lie, pure and simple.

As a result of that experience, I determined to find out as much as I could about other anti-Mormon literature. I was amazed at how much there was! My local Christian bookstore provided me with a number of books and tracts. I also spent several hours in the library of a local Bible college, Multnomah School of the Bible in Portland, Oregon, not far from my home. The shelves were filled with such material.

I should point out that by this time I had read the Book of Mormon several times. I had also spent many months studying and being enriched by the words of ancient and latter-day prophets. I knew Mormon church history quite well—from both Mormon and non-Mormon sources. My prior experience as an active Protestant gave me some additional insight into the world of sectarianism as well. In short, I approached my research with an open mind, but I was not unarmed.

This book is a report on my research and experiences. It is not meant to convert or convince anyone of the truth or validity of The Church of Jesus Christ of Latter-day Saints, even though I strongly believe in the Church's truthfulness and validity. My purpose is simply to help clear up common misconceptions about the Church and its doctrines and teachings. I hope also to give some insight into the sources and philosophies behind anti-Mormon material for the benefit of those who have encountered it and may have deep concerns or questions. Perhaps the results of my studies and experience will prove helpful to those who have been recently introduced to or are investigating the LDS Church and to those who are assisting others in their investigation of the Church.

A Historical Perspective

The Church of Jesus Christ of Latter-day Saints boldly proclaims that the gospel of Jesus Christ and the sacred authority to administer the ordinances of the gospel were taken from the earth shortly after the earthly ministry of the Lord Jesus Christ. The apostasy, or "falling away" (see 2 Thes. 2:3), from the true teachings of Jesus Christ is a matter of biblical prophecy and historical record.[2] It is an accepted matter of history that all the apostles ordained by Jesus Christ, with the exception of John the Revelator, were killed by enemies of the Church. Once these appointed servants were gone, no person on the earth could speak in the name of Christ nor had the authority to administer the ordinances of the gospel. Without the benefit of continual revelation from God to his appointed apostles and prophets (Amos 3:7), the children of men struggled to interpret and administer a correct theology. As a result, many doctrines and practices entered into the Church that were not in concert with the gospel of Jesus Christ as he established it. Simple principles of the gospel were mixed with pagan philosophical movements of the day.[3] Thus, the church of medieval times, which resulted from these changes in doctrines and ordinances, became less and less like the church that Jesus Christ established during his earthly ministry.

The Christian church became a political tool during the reign of Constantine the Great.[4] Lacking divine answers to theological questions, Constantine called more than three hundred bishops together at Nicaea (now in Turkey) in A.D. 325 to reach some theological and doctrinal conclusions. One purpose of this general council was to define who or what God is. There were many ideas presented and many disputes between the bishops; however, in the end they arrived at a compromise, known as the Nicene Creed. This creed became the standard for the church of that day and is the root of the traditional understanding of the nature of the Godhead.

Soon afterwards, the philosopher Augustine (A.D. 354–430), while studying the philosophies of the neoplatonists, was impressed to become a Christian and to work at defining and refining Christian beliefs. The ideas of "original sin" (and, therefore, the ordinance of infant baptism) and being saved wholly by the grace of God—and only at God's "good pleasure"—were not the contributions of Jesus Christ, but of Augustine.[5]

With the invention of the printing press in the mid-1400s, the Bible became available to many people who previously had been denied it. (Until then it was forbidden for anyone but a Catholic priest to have or to read the Bible.) As a result, people began to note distinct differences between Bible teachings and the policies and actions of the established church. People began to form their own ideas of how the gospel ought to be administered and interpreted. This became the foundation of the Reformation (A.D. 1500s), a "protest" (hence Protestant) movement that started with great reformers, especially Martin Luther (Lutheran) and John Calvin (Presbyterian and Puritan).[6]

Amidst this spirit of Protestant reform, King Henry VIII formed the Church of England in 1534 when the Pope refused to grant the king a divorce from his wife, Catherine of Aragon. In retaliation, Henry coerced Parliament to pass the Act of Supremacy, which made the king head of the Church in England and denounced the Pope. This act allowed people other than the Pope to reform the church's teachings and was the catalyst for further reformation by splinter groups attempting to restore the New Testament church. Later, in 1559, after many disputes as to whether the Church of England should be primarily Protestant or Catholic, Queen Elizabeth I effected a political compromise between the two prominent theologies and reinstated the Church of England. Today, a wide range of theological opinions are represented in these churches.

Within the various Protestant groups, there began to be widespread disagreement over points of doctrine, the form of liturgy, church government, and other issues. These disagreements led to the formation of many splinter denominations. For example, the Anglican Church broke away from the Church of England. Then a group of people called

Separatists, eventually called Congregationalists, broke away from the Anglican Church because they did not think they could reform the church from within. Another group of Separatists went to the Netherlands under the direction of John Smyth and became known as the Baptists. Later, in the 1700s, John Wesley, unable to reform the Anglican Church to his satisfaction, began the movement known today as the Methodists.

Some churches seemed to begin spontaneously. Pentecostal churches, for example, originated at revivals in 1901 at a Bible college in Topeka, Kansas, where people spoke in a language they had never learned (that is, they spoke "in tongues"). Today individual Pentecostal denominations differ greatly in interpretations of matters of faith and prophecy. As a result, there are now more than thirty separate Pentecostal denominations in the United States and Canada, each believing in its own approach to worship and evangelism.[7]

Some churches were formed by government acts. The United Church of Canada, established in 1925 following an act of Canadian Parliament, was originally a conglomeration of three theologies: Methodism, Presbyterianism, and Congregationalism. Another church, the Evangelical United Brethren Church, later joined the United Church of Canada.[8]

The above examples are only a small representation of the fragmenting and dividing of churches through reform. By the early 1800s, literally hundreds of churches had been organized to express the individual religious desires and biblical interpretations of the people. As these churches spread to other countries, further reformation produced groups that were markedly different from their parent religious groups. Even through the 1800s and into this century, religious division has continued. This division is a fulfillment of the prophesy in 2 Thessalonians that there would be a "falling away" from the church Christ established during his mortal ministry (2 Thes. 2:3).

It is interesting to review the attitudes and positions of the great reformers in relation to the movements their protestations founded. Did they seek to establish the one "true church"? Did they think they had the power to act in God's name and to administer the ordinances as clearly manifest by the apostles in the New Testament? They did not.

Martin Luther was surprised and disappointed to find that his efforts to reform the Roman Catholic Church had instead founded a new church. Moreover, he did not want his name on any church because he felt that the church should take its name only from Christ, yet this new church was named after him! Luther simply stated in his writings that he wanted to reform the church according to the holy scriptures and that the Catholic Church had failed in its responsibility to preserve Christianity.

First an Anglican priest, then a Puritan sympathizer, Roger Williams, founder of the state of Rhode Island and of the Baptist Church in the

Americas, was at heart, a separatist. He firmly believed that the authority to act in the name of God was taken from the earth and that none in his day held that sacred right. Williams had great faith in Jesus Christ and knew that He would not withdraw Himself from the world completely, but would, in time, send "new apostles to recover and restore all the ordinances and churches of Christ out of the ruins of antichristian apostasy."[9] He urged his followers to establish an environment that would permit God to "pour forth those fiery streams again of *tongues* and *prophecy* in the restoration of Zion."[10]

John Wesley, the founder of Methodism, was an ordained priest in the Church of England who tried to reform the church in accord with biblical principles. His Methodist societies were mere study groups within the Church of England until 1784 when Wesley was forced to begin his own sect in order to provide ministers to the Methodist societies in New England. Like Luther, Williams, and others, Wesley recognized that divine administrative authority had indeed been taken from the earth through apostasy. In his writings, Wesley states:

It does not appear that these extraordinary gifts of the Holy Ghost were common in the church for more than two or three centuries. We seldom hear of them after that fatal period when the Emperor Constantine called

himself a Christian. . . . The Christians had
no more of the Spirit of Christ than the other
heathens. . . . This was the real cause why the
extraordinary gifts of the Holy Ghost were no
longer to be found in the Christian church—
because the Christians were turned heathens
again, and had only a dead form left.[11]

After the passing of these and other reformers,
their churches were left in much the same state in
which they were founded; nevertheless, to
perpetuate their philosophies, each of these
religious organizations eventually established
colleges where those choosing a career in the
ministry could be trained. In these special
universities, students were taught the religious
dogma of their own faith—doctrine based on a
mixture of biblical scripture and the philosophies of
men. Once they had been trained for the ministry,
these new pastors went forth to expound their
individual interpretations and to win converts to
their unique brand of religious philosophy.

It is important to understand the distinction between truth and philosophy. There are many religious philosophies in the world. The universe of
Christian churches encompasses widespread differences on doctrinal points, ideas concerning worship, and requirements for salvation. Each of these
churches presents a separate religious philosophy.
For example, most popular Christian churches believe that accepting Christ is essential to personal

salvation, but some do not. Some churches believe
that infants as well as adults should be baptized.
Others say baptism is necessary only for adults. Still
others profess that baptism itself is unnecessary.
The list of philosophical differences, even within
mainline Christian churches, is extensive.

When any religious group or individual attacks
another, it is a war of philosophy, not a war of or
for truth. Claims that Mormon doctrine does not
conform to an established Protestant religious philosophy or to some traditional biblical interpretations are true indeed. This is because the LDS
Church is not a break-off of any church, as the Protestant churches are. Its doctrines are not based upon
the philosophies of men, but are God's revealed
truths. Keep in mind that a truthseeker is interested
in gaining truth and wisdom; he or she does not
seek a contest of religious opinion. The apostle Paul
said: "Beware lest any man spoil you through philosophy and vain deceit, after the tradition of men,
after the rudiments of the world, and not after
Christ" (Col. 2:8).

In 1820 in the midst of the aforementioned religious confusion, Joseph Smith, Jr., a fourteen-year-
old farm boy in upstate New York, was searching
among all the popular churches of the day in an
effort to find out which was the true church of Jesus
Christ. He visited many revivals and other meet-
ings, but he was confused at the contradictions he
heard declared as doctrines. While studying the
Bible one evening, Joseph was impressed by a

passage in James 1:5 that says wisdom may be obtained from God through prayer. After some considerable preparation, he decided he must "ask of God." In answer to his humble prayer, Joseph received a marvelous vision in which God the Father and Jesus Christ appeared to him. Their answer to him was clear: All the churches were wrong, and he should join none of them, for, in the words of the Savior, "they draw near to [God] with their lips, but their hearts are far from [Him], they teach for doctrines the commandments of men, having a form of godliness, but they deny the power thereof" (JSH 1:19). Joseph was also told that if he remained worthy, he would be instrumental in establishing the true church of Jesus Christ upon the earth again.

A few days after Joseph Smith received this vision, he was in the company of a Methodist minister and, while discussing religion, told the minister about his prayer and the vision he received. The cleric responded "with great contempt, saying [that the vision] was all of the devil, that . . . visions and revelations . . . [and] all such things had ceased with the apostles, and that there would never be any more of them" (JSH 1:21).[12]

Joseph was treated harshly by all the religious leaders in his community because of his testimony of his vision. In his history, Joseph explained:

It seems as though the adversary was aware, at a very early period of my life, that I was destined to prove a disturber and an annoyer of his kingdom; else why should the powers of darkness combine against me? Why the opposition and persecution that arose against me, almost in my infancy? . . .

My telling the story had excited a great deal of prejudice against me among professors of religion, and was the cause of great persecution, which continued to increase; and though I was an obscure boy, only between fourteen and fifteen years of age, and my circumstances in life such as to make a boy of no consequence in the world, yet men of high standing would take notice sufficient to excite the public mind against me, and create a bitter persecution; and this was common among all the sects—all united to persecute me. (JSH 1:20, 22)

The persecutions described by the Prophet Joseph Smith in the early days following his wondrous vision grew in number and intensified as the work Joseph had been given went forth. He was beaten, tarred and feathered, and jailed under hideous circumstances for long periods of time. He was unjustly accused, tried, and condemned by false witnesses and driven from town to town and from place to place. Above all, he was forced to stand by and watch as the people who believed in the restoration of the gospel of Jesus Christ through him were treated in like manner—all in the name of religion. Finally, he was murdered, along with his beloved brother Hyrum, by a mob of over one hundred rifle-bearing, blacken-faced men, while the two men were supposedly under the "protection" of the law at the city jail in Carthage, Illinois.

After the death of the Prophet Joseph Smith, the sacred authority to act as the mouthpiece of God and chief administrator of the kingdom of God on earth was immediately transferred to Brigham Young, the next senior apostle of the Church. At Brigham Young's death in 1877, the keys of authority were passed instantly to the next senior apostle, John Taylor, and so on. So, since the moment Joseph Smith was ordained a prophet of God and president of the Church, there has been a prophet on the earth to give divine guidance to the children of men.

Discovering Truth from the Source

The Church of Jesus Christ of Latter-day Saints is one of the fastest growing religious movements in the world today. While mainstream Protestant churches are recording annual reductions in church activity, the LDS Church enjoys a membership increasing by hundreds of thousands annually. Membership of the Church worldwide is approaching ten million.

Incident to the continuing growth of the Church is an increase in attacks on latter-day doctrines, the Prophet Joseph Smith, the Book of Mormon, and other Church teachings. Initially, as has been historically documented, this persecution of the Church involved house-burning, rape, murder, and ultimately driving the Saints to the western United States in the mid-1800s—all done by hostile political and mob actions. During that period many Church members lost their lives either by direct persecution or by the hardships forced upon them as they were driven west.

Today the persecutions leveled at the Church have taken a subtle, pseudointellectual approach. As I mentioned earlier, I have made a serious study of the literature that fuels such persecution. Having read a great deal of anti-Mormon literature, I have seen interesting patterns in these writers' attacks. Non-Mormon religious leaders have commented on the booklets and pamphlets they have received from the various anti-Mormon ministries, describing them as in general of a low caliber and exhibiting a definite bias. They remark that this material has little scientific or theological merit.

Anti-Mormon authors commonly print rumor or opinion, mixed with proven facts or truth. Moreover, if you read the bibliography of anti-Mormon books, you will find that the authors often make reference to other anti-Mormon writings without regard to how vulgar or unsubstantiated the referenced writings may be. This interrelated recycling of untruth and prejudice indicates that the motives of such authors are to sell books, to preserve their own flawed philosophies, or to cast doubt on others' beliefs. It would seem that truth, charity, and understanding—all necessary parts of a true Christian character—are not high priorities to them.

I have often wondered why anti-Mormon authors did not consult Latter-day Saint references in any detail or in full context. Why not ask a local or general LDS Church leader about points of doctrine or belief? Why, with access to the scriptures and to thousands of LDS discourses, do they focus on the minutia and interpret these relatively insignificant pieces of data incorrectly? If you wanted to know about the character of Christ, would you accept the statements of the Roman guard at the sepulchre? Or of the blood-stained Pharisee who rejoiced at the death of the Savior? Or the anti-

Christians'? I think not. Why, then, do anti-Mormon writers consistently accept the testimonies of those who murdered the prophet, or of those who are apostates or bitter enemies of the Church or both? In my opinion, those who heed these anti-Mormon authors' lies are simply not interested in the truth.

In all this, there remain questions and challenges that are disturbing or thought provoking. In this book I have attempted to catalog the most popular pronouncements and questions of the anti-Mormon movement. I've tried to give a brief, factual response, as well as references for more information on the specified topic (see also Suggested Reading List, page 106).

Our Heavenly Father knew that Satan would sow seeds of doubt and confusion in the world and thus obscure access to eternal blessings for His children. Our God is a loving Father who wants His children to know the truth and to achieve their celestial potential. But there are so many voices trying to be heard and so many confusing doctrines being taught. How is one to know the truth?

James 1:5 of the Holy Bible reads: "If any of you lack wisdom, let him ask of God, that giveth to all *men* liberally, and upbraideth not; and it shall be given him." In Matthew 7:7 the Lord adds: "Ask, and it shall be given you; seek, and ye shall find; knock, and it shall be opened unto you." Later, in verse 11, Jesus explains that we naturally want to give good gifts to our children. Then he says, "How much more shall your Father which is in heaven give good things to them that ask him?" In the Book of Mormon, a great prophet and leader said, as a part of his humble prayer: "O Lord, thou hast given us a commandment that we must call upon thee, that from thee we may receive according to our desires" (BM, Ether 3:2).

Finally, in the closing chapter of the Book of Mormon, the prophet Moroni writes: "And when ye shall receive these things, I would exhort you that ye would ask God, the Eternal Father, in the name of Christ, if these things are not true; and if ye shall ask with a sincere heart, with real intent, having faith in Christ, he will manifest the truth of it unto you, by the power of the Holy Ghost" (BM, Moroni 10:4).

The Lord's message and commandment is clear. We need not depend on the words of others to ascertain truth. Once we study it out in our minds, we can go to God, the source of *all* truth. When we ask in faith, with a pure heart, he has promised to give us wisdom and verify truth. Ultimately, we must all come to terms with this important formula and then gain our own witnesses of the truthfulness of God's works. A personal testimony, born of the Spirit, is the only unfailing source of truth. In 1 John 5:9 it says: "If we receive the witness of men, the witness of God is greater: for this is the witness of God which he hath testified of his Son."

At one point in his ministry, Jesus asked his disciples: "Whom do men say that I the Son of man am?" (Matt. 16:13). The disciples responded with various opinions of the day. Jesus then asked: "But whom say ye that I am?" (Matt. 16:15). Simon Peter instantly replied: "Thou art the Christ, the Son of the living God" (Matt. 16:16). Jesus then blessed Peter and added: "Flesh and blood hath not revealed *it* unto thee, but my Father which is in heaven" (Matt. 16:17). Peter had received his divine witness from God the Father, not from anything he had heard, experienced, or learned from men. We must also receive our testimonies from God. No earthly source will do. Reading and pondering the scriptures can enrich our minds and hearts. Living gospel principles will give us peace and joy. But a sure knowledge and witness comes only as a manifestation from our Father in Heaven.

If anyone ever tries to tell you that you cannot receive divine answers to life's most compelling and vital questions, you may know that that person—regardless of relation, title, or credential—is trying to deceive you.

The Church of Jesus Christ of Latter-day Saints declares in its Articles of Faith that all people should be free to worship God according to their own beliefs. Missionaries and members of the Church can and should be active in proclaiming the news of the restored gospel and encouraging everyone to investigate and learn of the blessings available to them. This activity, or mission, is not an attack on the religious beliefs of any person or sect but an invitation to partake of the fulness of the gospel of Jesus Christ. Those who refuse to listen or choose not to heed the message are treated with respect and consideration.

The Lord gives us a specific responsibility to test and try new ideas, and through his prophets, he gives us guidelines for making sound judgments. First Thessalonians 5:19–21 reads: "Quench not the Spirit. Despise not prophesyings. Prove all things; hold fast that which is good." What, then, should be the Christian response to other religions? What should we do if we are fearful of being deceived?

We need look no further than the Bible to learn what the proper Christian attitude and response to any new and seemingly different religious movements should be. Acts 5 in the New Testament gives a formula for dealing with any person or group whose beliefs differ from our own.

In that record the chief priests were in council to determine what should be done with Peter and the other apostles who were preaching with him. They had been preaching this new religion about Jesus Christ. Because the doctrine taught by Peter was different from the priests' traditions and because people were believing the apostles' words, the priests had the apostles thrown into prison. An angel delivered the apostles from the prison, but they were returned to stand before the council to be tried once again.

After Peter bore his apostolic witness of Jesus Christ to the council, "then stood there up one in the council, a Pharisee, named Gamaliel, a doctor of the law, had in reputation among all the people, and commanded to put the apostles forth a little space; And said unto them, Ye men of Israel, take heed to yourselves what ye intend to do as touching these men. . . . Refrain from these men, and let them alone: for if this counsel or this work be of men, it will come to nought: But if it be of God, ye cannot overthrow it; lest haply ye be found even to fight against God" (Acts 5:34–5; 38–9).

We know that the works of darkness will always ultimately fail. Those who work to deceive others will be frustrated, and their works will come to nothing.

A modern-day prophet, President Spencer W. Kimball, said the following about truth:

> Th[ere] is an absolute truth! . . . It is as true as the near-spherical shape of the earth, and as absolute as gravity; as true as the shining of the sun—as positive as the truth that we live. Most of the world disbelieves it; ministers attempt to disprove it; intellectuals think to rationalize it out of existence; but when all the people of the world are dead, and the ministers and priests are ashes, and the highly trained are mouldering in their graves, the truth will go forward—the Church will continue triumphant and the gospel will still be true. . . .
>
> Opinions? Of course, there is a difference of opinion; but again opinions cannot change

laws or absolute truths! Opinions will never make the earth to be flat, the sun to dim its light, God to die, or the Savior to cease being the Son of God.

[I testify to you that His church has been restored to the earth.] This is not another church. This is *the* church. This is not another gospel or philosophy. This is the church and gospel of Jesus Christ. [13]

Because of the restoration of the gospel of Jesus Christ to the earth once again, the truths that we need to know to enable us to live so that we can return back to our Father in Heaven are available to us. By following this gospel, individuals can have more understanding, more happiness, more peace of mind, and more blessings than they have ever before had. There is only one way to obtain all of these blessings—by following the plan of our Heavenly Father that has been restored in our day through the Prophet Joseph Smith.

Pronouncements and Questions

The following are responses to some common pronouncements of anti-Mormons and questions about Mormon doctrine, history, practices, and so forth. The responses are in no way exhaustive; I have tried to provide enough material to clarify or correct the fallacious claims and to give references for further information about Mormon beliefs.

Mormons practice polygamy

Here is a statement that was once true but is often overplayed, misunderstood, and sensationalized by detractors. The facts are that during a period of early Church history, the law of plural marriage was practiced by a small portion of Church members. Before anyone overreacts to that admission, it would be well to remember two points:

(1) Plural marriage has been practiced throughout the ages for short periods of time when directed by the Lord for his purposes, as in the cases of Abraham, Isaac, Jacob, and others.

(2) Joseph Smith, Jr., by his sacred calling, held the keys and the authority, as a part of the promised restoration of all things, to exercise this principle when so directed by the

Lord. Joseph Smith said, "I hold the keys of this power in the last days; for there is never but one on earth at a time on whom the power and its keys are conferred; *and I have constantly said no man shall have but one wife at a time, unless the Lord directs otherwise.*"[14]

So, why did some early Mormons practice plural marriage? Simply because they were commanded to do so by God through His prophet. In Mormon doctrine, plural marriage is not an essential principle of the gospel, nor is it preferable to monogamy. The Lord, however, may choose to command, forbid, or tolerate this practice among his people as he deems it necessary or appropriate. Indeed, he has done all three![15] A professor at Brigham Young University, Stephen E. Robinson, wrote:

> In Western culture plural marriage is generally abhorred, but the roots of this abhorrence can hardly be described as biblical, for the Old Testament explicitly sanctions polygamy, and the New Testament does not forbid it. The practice could not have been abhorrent to Jesus and the first-century Jewish Christians, for their culture was not Western, and plural marriage was sanctioned in the law of Moses, the holiness of which was endorsed by both Jesus and Paul.[16]

Far from being a whoredom or sordid practice, polygamy was governed by strict limits, order, and mutual agreement, when entering into and, if necessary, terminating the practice. Those who entered into polygamy were pure in heart and strictly virtuous. Those who perverted or abused the system received immediate and heavy condemnation.

Even the early Christians saw that polygamy was a custom not out of harmony with the church. Saint Augustine, the great philosopher and Catholic convert who became the Bishop of Hippo, responded to the church's condemnation of polygamy: "Jacob the son of Isaac is charged with having committed a great crime because he had four wives. But here there is no ground for a criminal accusation: for a plurality of wives was no crime when it was the custom; and it is a crime now, because it is no longer the custom. . . . The only reason of its being a crime now to do this, is because custom and the laws forbid it."[17] The same was true of the early LDS Church.

In 1890 President Wilford Woodruff, then the prophet of the Church, issued the Manifesto, as directed by the Lord, commanding the practice of plural marriage to cease because antipolygamy legislation threatened to confiscate Church property, including the holy temples. Today all who engage in plural marriage are guilty of great wickedness, because God forbids the practice, and are subject to excommunication from the Church.

Mormonism is a cult

First, let's define *cult*. According to the *World Book Encyclopedia*, a cult is a "religious group devoted to a living leader, a new teaching, or an unusual practice."[18] In that sense Jesus Christ was the leader of a cult (the Christians), as far as the Jews were concerned. By the same token, Martin Luther was the leader of a cult, and Methodists, Presbyterians, and Baptists were cults when they began their reformed movements. All these groups have developed into organized churches.

Those who use the word *cult* to describe the organization or the members of The Church of Jesus Christ of Latter-day Saints do so for the sensational effect it may have on those who read their material. It is an effort to degrade Mormon doctrine or to imply that, as a cult, Mormons are not to be taken seriously, but are to be avoided or openly disdained.

Mormonism is a vital, living church where the gospel of Jesus Christ is taught in its fulness. There are no secret oaths required for membership in the LDS Church, and no unseemly practices or rituals are performed by its members. Members are free to remove themselves from Church activity at any time. Service and activity in the Church are free from compulsion and coercion in any form.

Mormons are not Christian

The testimony and confession that Jesus is the Christ is as central to Mormon doctrine as it is to any mainline Christian faith (perhaps even more so). However, accepting Mormons as Christian is difficult for some religious faiths—particularly for those who profess that "accepting Christ as our Savior" is all that matters and that this pronouncement alone qualifies an individual for ultimate heavenly rewards. For this group of believers, the Mormon testimony of Christ is not acceptable.[19] As a result, some groups go to great lengths to demonstrate how Mormons worship a "different Jesus Christ" from the one "true Christians" worship, and therefore, Mormons cannot be called "Christians."

History affirms that Catholic and Protestant denominations commonly claimed that other churches were not Christian. Now, after over five hundred years, they have become used to each other and, for the most part, accept each other in the "family of Christ," or as fellow Christians, regardless of the fact that they still disagree on many doctrinal issues. Since Mormonism is a relatively new Christian religion, Latter-day Saints have not been included in this "family of Christ" and have often been labeled "non-Christian."

The term *Christian* is only mentioned three times in the Bible, and it is never defined; however, *Webster's Third New International Dictionary* defines a Christian as "one who believes or professes or is assumed to believe in Jesus Christ and the truth as taught by him."[20] By this definition, The Church of Jesus Christ of Latter-day Saints— through declaration, practice, and worship—qualifies as a Christian church.

In his book *Mormon Doctrine*, the late Bruce R. McConkie, LDS apostle and respected Church scholar, said this in a short prelude to a comprehensive statement of belief regarding the Savior:

> As far as man is concerned, all things center in *Christ*. He is the Firstborn of the Father. By obedience and devotion to the truth he attained that pinnacle of intelligence which ranked him as a God, as the Lord Omnipotent, while yet in his [premortal] state. As such he became, under the Father, the Creator of this earth and of worlds without number; and he was then chosen to work out the infinite and eternal atonement, to come to this particular earth as the literal Son of the Father, and to put the whole plan of redemption, salvation, and exaltation in operation.
>
> Through him the gospel, all saving truths, and every edifying principle have been revealed in all ages. He is the Eternal Jehovah, the promised Messiah, the Redeemer and Savior, the Way, the Truth, and the Life. By him immortality and eternal life

become realities, and through his grace and goodness salvation is possible for all who will believe and obey.[21]

Members of the LDS Church worship the Jesus Christ who created this earth (see BofM, 1 Nephi 17:36; 2 Nephi 2:1–15; Bible, John 1:1–3), who was born of the Virgin Mary, and whose earthly ministry produced the gospel in its fulness. Latter-day Saints worship him who died on the cross at Calvary and rose on the third day to be seen of many, and who lives yet today. Mormons are members of his Church and kingdom, and they anxiously and hopefully await his promised return.[22]

Mormons worship a plurality of Gods

Latter-day Saints believe in one supreme God. He is God the Father. Associated with the Father are his Son Jesus Christ and the Holy Ghost.[23] These three constitute the Godhead, the governing council of the universe. The personages in this Trinity are distinct personalities, but they are as one because they are united in all things of faith and action. In *Mormon Doctrine*, Bruce R. McConkie wrote:

Though each God in the Godhead is a personage, separate and distinct from each of the others, yet they are "one God," meaning that they are united as one in the attributes of perfection. For instance, each has the fulness of truth, knowledge, charity, power, justice, judgment, mercy, and faith. Accordingly they all think, act, speak, and are alike in all things; and yet they are three separate and distinct entities. Each occupies space and is and can be in but one place at one time, but each has power and influence that is everywhere present. The oneness of the Gods is the same unity that should exist among the saints. (John 17; [BM] 3 Ne[phi] 28:10–11.)[24]

Joseph Smith said in a sermon on the subject of plurality of Gods:

The doctrine of a plurality of Gods is as prominent in the Bible as any other doctrine. . . . There are Gods many and Lords many . . . but to us there is but one God—that is *pertaining to us*, . . . and we are to be in subjection to that one.[25]

Mormons believe they will become gods

Latter-day Saints, on the basis of biblical teaching and inspired modern-day revelation, constantly seek personal righteousness and progression. This improvement not only involves establishing the

kingdom of God on the earth, but it is a pattern for
eternity. Our Father in Heaven has given us the
commandment to be perfect (Matt. 5:48). Such perfection implies that upon reaching a perfect state,
we will be like our Father in Heaven. Paul's teachings to the Romans are even more instructive. In
Romans 8:16–17 it reads: "The Spirit itself beareth
witness with our spirit, that we are the children of
God: And if children, then heirs; heirs of God, and
joint-heirs with Christ; if so be that we suffer with
him, that we may be also glorified together." Paul is
teaching the vital truth that we are children of God
and that we can, through our choices, which often
bring the above-mentioned suffering, and through
the grace of Christ, be heirs of the kingdom of God
(see D&C 86:9)—even on the same level, as joint-
heirs, with Jesus Christ. That is what Mormons
believe.

Mormons are not the only people who believe
that man is progressing towards godhood. a great
writer and Protestant theologian, C. S. Lewis, wrote:

The command *Be ye perfect* is not ideal-
istic gas. Nor is it a command to do the impossible. He is going to make us into
creatures that can obey that command. He
said (in the Bible) that we were "gods" and
He is going to make good His words. If we let
Him—for we can prevent Him, if we
choose—He will make the feeblest and filthi-
est of us into a god or goddess, dazzling,

radiant, immortal creature, pulsating all
through with such energy and joy and wisdom and love as we cannot now imagine, a
bright stainless mirror which reflects back to
God perfectly . . . His own boundless power
and delight and goodness. The process will be
long and in parts very painful; but that is
what we are in for. Nothing less. He meant
what He said.[26]

Our state after death is not an either/or proposi-
tion. Each individual is accorded a degree of glory
that is commensurate with his or her faith in Jesus
Christ and willingness to follow the commandments of God; thus, each of God's children receives
that which he or she is *willing* to receive. Some, because of their worthiness, will inherit "all that [the]
Father hath" (D&C 84:38). When you have all that
the Father has, then you are as the Father is.

Moreover, the doctrine of eternal progression, as
it has been revealed by the Lord through his appointed prophets, tells us that the work of the Lord
goes on beyond this life. Our capacity to learn and
grow and be productive after this life will be en-
hanced according to our earthly preparation. Family
relationships will be eternal; husband and wives
can be married, or sealed together, forever. Children can be sealed to parents in an unending relationship. No loved one need be lost or parted
from us for eternity! This glorious message is what
Paul made reference to when he said: "O death,

where *is* thy sting? O grave, where *is* thy victory?"
(1 Cor. 15:55).

Mormons believe in modern prophets and in continuing revelation

Yes, this is true. Mormons believe God has established a prophet on the earth today who gives
guidance and direction for our lives and for the
Church, through modern revelation. The Church
of Jesus Christ of Latter-day Saints is founded on
revelation. The prophet, possessing all the keys of
the priesthood, acts as president of the Church, and
the presidency presides over the Church and directs
its affairs. Joseph Smith said, "Revelations of the
mind and will of God to the Church, are to come
through the Presidency. This is the order of heaven,
and the power and privilege of this Priesthood. It is
also the privilege of any officer in this Church to
obtain revelations, so far as relates to his particular
calling and duty in the Church."[27] Thus, anyone can
receive revelation, according to his or her steward-
ship, for revelation is "making known the divine
truth by communication from the heavens."[28]

Elder Bruce R. McConkie wrote:

Devout persons of all Christian faiths
readily accepted the truth that revelation was
poured out upon the faithful, from age to
age, from Adam to the days of Christ's apos-

tles. They suppose, however, that since the apostolic era the heavens have been sealed and that revelation has ceased. In reality souls are just as precious in the sight of God today as they ever were, and revelation is still poured out in abundance so that souls may be led to salvation.[29]

As it says in Amos, "Surely the Lord GOD will do nothing, but he revealeth his secret unto his servants the prophets" (BM, Amos 3:7). It is a wonderful thing to be able to confidently follow the words of a living prophet, knowing those words come from God through revelation.

Mormons worship Joseph Smith

Worship is paying respect or homage to a divine being or supernatural power.[30] "Deity is worshiped in prayer, song, sermon, and testimony; by making covenants, offering sacrifices, performance of ordinances, and the participation in religious rituals and ceremonies."[31] Latter-day Saints worship God the Father and His Son, Jesus Christ, in this way (see "Mormons worship a plurality of gods," page 32).[32] Mormons do not consider Joseph Smith to be deity, nor do they worship him in any way or perform any worshipful actions toward him. President Gordon B. Hinckley stated:

We do not worship the Prophet [Joseph Smith]. We worship God our Eternal Father, and the risen Lord Jesus Christ. But we acknowledge [Joseph Smith], we proclaim him, we respect him, we reverence him as an instrument in the hands of the Almighty in restoring to the earth the ancient truth of the divine gospel.[33]

Faithful members of the Church hold Joseph Smith to be a prophet of God in the same sense as they believe the prophets of the Old Testament were prophets of God. Anyone who has read any of the revelations received by Joseph Smith, or who has read from the Book of Mormon to any degree, will see the emphasis on the worship of one true God and of His Son, Jesus the Christ. Anyone who has attended a Mormon worship service will be impressed by the focus on the Savior in all worship, conversation, and study.

As a faithful Latter-day Saint, I have tremendous admiration and respect for this great latter-day prophet, Joseph Smith. The persecution he endured in his short life and the sacrifices he made for the benefit of others are astonishing to me. I know of Joseph's great love for Jesus Christ and His teachings. I have come to appreciate the nobility of Joseph's actions, even toward those who fought against him and sought to destroy him with their fallacious reports. He was a man of great spiritual strength who withstood hardships with a cheerful heart. Those who denounce Joseph Smith as a liar or a fraud, or who suggest that he was simply a charlatan bent on his own aggrandizement, pronounce their own ignorance, for many great men who knew the "boy prophet" testified of his honorable and impressive character.

I know that he was not a perfect man. Joseph was chastised by the Lord in revelations more than any other person. He knew he was not a perfect man—he said and wrote so on many occasions. I do not expect him to be perfect. Yet I revere Joseph Smith as the Lord's mouthpiece and a prophet of the last dispensation.

While he was a prominent Presbyterian minister, Roger R. Keller (now LDS) carefully studied the life and teachings of Joseph Smith and wrote:

Joseph Smith's desire and ability to provide (based upon a literalistic interpretation of the King James scriptures) theological responses to the innumerable doctrinal questions with which we all struggle was truly amazing. We may ultimately disagree with the results of his exegesis, but we must respect him as a Christian of immense stature whose legacy to the world is a Church whose membership now numbers in excess of 5 million persons [currently nearly ten million].[34]

Like Paul of old, Joseph Smith was keenly aware of his shortcomings and weaknesses, but he was also very aware of his divine calling and the eternal implications of his assigned ministry. A balanced review of the life and teachings of Joseph Smith reveals a man of great stature, richly deserving of the honor bestowed upon him by those who knew him well.

What about the various accounts of Joseph Smith's first vision?

Joseph Smith's first vision in 1820, wherein he beheld God the Father and Jesus Christ, is one of the most significant religious events in the history of the world. This glorious vision restored the fulness of the gospel to the earth and established a new prophet to lead God's children out of darkness.

Since this pivotal event is so central to the restored gospel, it is no wonder that the anti-Mormons would target Joseph's different descriptions of this experience and look for reasons to discredit or cast doubt.

Specifically, there are four accounts of the First Vision, the first recorded in 1832, twelve years after the experience. The other three versions followed in 1835, 1838, and 1842. It is important to note that these successive accounts were not written to "update" or "correct" the original account, but were simply reports of the event given under different circumstances. Each account was recorded by a different scribe from a different perspective and for a different purpose. As a result, they emphasize various aspects of Joseph's experience.

One reason Joseph's account of his First Vision varied in content is that there was so much to tell! In his most complete account (written in 1838) the Prophet concluded: "Many other things did [the Savior] say unto me, which I cannot write at this time" (JSH 1:20).

Anti-Mormon writers commonly claim that Joseph's "numerous" accounts of the First Vision cast doubt on the prophet's integrity and on the validity of the event itself.[35] However, the basic truths disclosed in each account are in complete harmony. The differences that do exist are simple grammatical changes or observations that show different facets of the same event. In fact, the subtle differences in Joseph's accounts help to support the integrity of Joseph's experience. It is a clear indication that Joseph did not simply memorize a story and pass it along in exact detail.

On the other hand, contradictions in scripture are not as uncommon as some religious leaders would have us believe. To demonstrate this, one could compare the accounts of the Savior's life and teachings by the authors of the four Gospels. Each was an eye witness to Jesus' expressions and miracles, but each recorded those events differently. The accounts about the experience in Gethsemane and the resurrection are recorded by these apostles, but each account disagrees on such details as the number of angels present and whether they were standing or sitting, and on the number of women present at the tomb.

Consider also the description of the conversion of the apostle Paul on the road to Damascus. Paul's accounts in Acts 22 and 26 differ in detail from Luke's account in Acts 9. In Acts 9:7 we read that those traveling with Paul heard a voice but saw no man. But in Acts 22:9 it tells us that Paul's fellow travelers saw a light but heard no voice. These biblical accounts seem to conflict. In another example of apparent contradiction from the Bible, the description in Matthew 27:5 of Judas Iscariot's death is different from that in Acts 1:18. How do we deal with these inconsistencies? Disbelievers scoff the Bible for its conflicting reports; believers recognize the value of the great realities that are taught—Christ's tomb was *empty*! Paul received a miraculous vision from the resurrected Lord! And Judas died an ignominious death for his betrayal!

The central message of Joseph Smith's accounts of his vision did not vary. The differences in details were a result of having an enormously significant message that issued from an equally complex and astounding experience. There was more than he could take in and certainly more than he could relate. That which survives today as the official version of the Prophet Joseph Smith's first vision (i.e., the account found in Joseph Smith—History [PGP]) is in complete harmony with earlier versions. In no instance has the basic message changed concerning the historical setting of the truths unfolded during this remarkable event. What changes have been made were made in an effort to convey, in the clearest language possible, the truths unfolded by God.

Joseph Smith took the Book of Mormon from a manuscript written by Solomon Spaulding.

The Spaulding Manuscript is a fictional story published in 1885 when it was found, about seventy years after the death of its author. The story is about a group of Romans who, while sailing to England early in the fourth century A.D., were blown off course and landed in North America. One of these Romans kept a history of their experiences among the eastern American Indian tribes.

The first to assert that a direct connection existed between the Book of Mormon and the Spaulding Manuscript was "Doctor" Philastus Hurlbut, who was excommunicated from the Church in 1833 for repeated acts of immorality. Desiring to discredit the Mormons, Hurlbut set out to harm the reputation of Joseph Smith and the Book of Mormon. In 1834 Hurlbut collaborated with Eber D. Howe, a newspaper publisher, in preparing an anti-Mormon publication, *Mormonism Unvailed* [sic] (see pages 76–77 and 87–91 for more on Hurlbut and Howe). When the Spaulding Manuscript was found in 1884 and it was clear that the Book of Mormon did not in any way derive from it, Howe speculated that Spaulding must have written another manuscript that served as the source of the Book of Mormon. This other "lost" manuscript has never surfaced, and no other writings of Spaulding have ever been found.

By the 1840s the so-called "Spaulding theory" had become the main anti-Mormon explanation for the Book of Mormon. When the original Spaulding manuscript was found in 1884, it was promptly published by the Latter-day Saints to refute the Spaulding theory. No serious student of Mormonism gives credibility to the Spaulding Manuscript theory.

In 1980 a trio of anti-Mormon writers published a book documenting professional graphologist statements that indicated similarities between Spaulding's handwriting and one of the scribes of the Book of Mormon, thus reopening the Solomon Spaulding controversy.[36] Further research into the matter showed that these anti-Mormons had been too hasty in their conclusions. The graphologists involved repudiated statements published in this book, claiming them false and misleading. Moreover, upon examination of original documents by these handwriting experts, it was determined that no handwriting connection exists between Spaulding and the Book of Mormon scribe.

If the Book of Mormon is inspired scripture, why have so many changes been made to it?

This question casts doubt upon the authenticity of the Book of Mormon by insinuating that major changes have been made to its message or meaning. Research will show this to be an empty claim. The translation of the Book of Mormon was a miracle accomplished by "the power of God" (D&C 1:29). Joseph did not give details about the actual process of translation, except to say that he dictated the words as they were rendered from the ancient text to one of several scribes. The resulting manuscript was thus the product of Joseph's spoken words as written down by a recorder. Since spelling and grammar were not standardized in the early 1800s, many variations in phonetic expression needed to be corrected in the first edition. For example, words in 1 Nephi 7:20 were changed from "ware sorraful" to "were sorrowful" in the first edition. In 1 Nephi 13:23 the word "plaits" was changed to "plates," and so on. Literally hundreds of such changes had to be made to the 464-page manuscript prior to publication.[37]

In 1830 the first edition of the Book of Mormon was printed in Palmyra, New York. The typesetter and text compositor provided most of the punctuation and paragraphing for the first edition. Here again, because typesetting was a slow and laborious manual task, many errors were made. Some errors were even corrected in the first press run, necessitating editing and further correction. As in any publication (especially one with multiple print-ings—current text included) corrections during transcription, editing, and so forth are all a natural part of the literary process. Moreover, putting into men's languages the words of God is undoubtedly the most difficult literary task of all. Elder Robert J. Matthews wrote:

> The Prophet Joseph Smith was well aware of this problem. During his lifetime, three editions of the Book of Mormon were printed. Each time, he amended the text in a few places to more correctly convey the in-tended meaning of his translation. Other changes in these and successive editions were made to correct typographical errors, improper spelling, and inaccurate or missing punctuation and to improve grammar and sentence structure to eliminate ambiguity. None of these changes, individually or col-lectively, alters the message of the Book of Mormon.[38]

Since that time, after careful and prayerful con-sideration by those who held the special authority to do so, other changes were made that smoothed the message and clarified the meaning or intent of various phrases. Even in the 1981 version, such changes were made.[39]

Some people ignore the central focus and the pure examples of Christian teachings contained in the Book of Mormon, concentrating on minor changes made to the text in various printings over 150 years—changes meant to clarify and simplify difficult passages. It is important to note that despite changes that have been made to the spelling, punctuation, and text of the Book of Mormon since its translation,[40] the central message has remained unaltered. It still stands as the most correct of all scriptures.

The Book of Mormon is an open book, available to all for their individual enlightenment and research. Millions of people throughout the world have gained a witness of the divine nature of the Lord Jesus Christ and his restored gospel by reading this inspired scripture. It is truly a companion to the Holy Bible and another witness for Jesus Christ.

Dee Jay Nelson claimed that the Pearl of Great Price was incorrectly translated by Joseph Smith.

The Pearl of Great Price is a sacred volume of scripture and is one of the four LDS standard works (or canonized scriptures). The two main books of this scripture, the books of Moses and Abraham, were translated by Joseph Smith from original ancient documents. The method of translation is unknown. We only know that it was accomplished by the power of God, as was the Book of Mormon.

Dee Jay Nelson claimed to be a professor, a doctor (with a Ph.D. in Egyptology), and a renowned Egyptologist. He gave lectures to any group who would pay his fees. During his lectures he convincingly but falsely maintained that he was given special permission by the LDS Church to translate the original documents of the Pearl of Great Price. This claim breaks down in several places. First, Nelson could not have studied the "original" of the book of Abraham. The original papyri of the Pearl of Great Price had long been lost. Only fragments remain. Those papyri that were in the possession of the LDS Church were but a small part of the original collection, and the book of Abraham papyri were not among them. Moreover, upon receiving the remains of the Pearl of Great Price papyri from the Metropolitan Museum, the Church placed the fragments on public display and welcomed scholars to examine them. No one was commissioned to make an official translation.

Nelson's "professional" translation of the fragments produced quite a different result from that of the Prophet Joseph Smith—once Nelson discovered how lucrative his lies were, he changed from agreeing with the Prophet's translations to disagreeing. (As it turns out, Nelson could not translate Egyptian without the help of a real Egyptologist.)

Nelson was completely exposed in 1981 by Robert L. and Rosemary Brown in their book *They Lie in Wait to Deceive: A Study of Anti-Mormon Deception*, vol. 1. However, anti-Mormon writers, including "Doctor" Walter Martin, Wayne L. Cowdrey, Howard A. Davis, Donald R. Scales, Jerald and Sandra Tanner, Harry D. Ropp, H. Michael Marquardt, and Father William J. Mitchell, continue to make extensive use of Nelson's fables in their writings. (See page 97 for more on Nelson.)

What about Joseph Smith's false prophecies?

This question primarily springs from an anti-Mormon accusation using a misreading of Deuteronomy 18:22 to discredit Joseph Smith. This scripture tells the people how they can know if a prophet is speaking in the name of the Lord or if he is speaking "presumptuously"—that is, boldly of his own views. The Lord says, if what the prophet says fails to come to pass, it was not of the Lord, and they need not concern themselves with it, or "be afraid of him," as the Lord puts it. In his book *How to Answer a Mormon*, Robert Morey, making reference to this scripture, writes: "The logic of this biblical passage is very simple. If someone claims to be a prophet of God but his predictions fail to happen, this person is a false prophet."[41]

Well, that is not what this scripture says at all. The scripture never says the man is a "false prophet"; it says the thing that the prophet said was not a prophecy from the Lord and is not binding on the people. In fact, the scripture explicitly says "when *a prophet* speaketh" and "*the prophet* hath spoken" (emphasis added). But a misinterpretation does not stop Morey from building an entire book on that premise anyway. (Morey demonstrates how creative people can be in interpreting scripture and how word games can be used to deceive.)

In truth, Joseph Smith gave no false prophecies; however, some people have chosen to misquote him, take his words out of context, misinterpret his writings, and draw conclusions that are unsubstantiated and in some cases, incredible in the extreme. Many people, both friendly and unfriendly to Joseph Smith, have recorded statements he made at various times in his life. Unsubstantiated personal journals, histories, and meeting notes where the prophet supposedly said one thing or another are sometimes put forth as false prophecies by enemies of the Church. I've heard and seen many such claims and researched as many as I could when original documentation was available (it seldom was). When dealing with the sanctioned, canonized writings of Joseph Smith, anti-Mormons have little to work with indeed. Their response is to be very creative.

A typical example of a prophecy received by Joseph Smith that anti-Mormons claim is false is found in Doctrine and Covenants 130. In this scripture the Lord reveals many eternal principles and truths that had been lost to the world until Joseph Smith restored them. This is also the revelation in which the Lord revealed the beginning of the great Civil War in the United States. This prophecy states:

I prophesy, in the name of the Lord God, that the commencement of the difficulties which will cause much bloodshed previous to the coming of the Son of Man will be in South Carolina.

It may probably arise through the slave question. This a voice declared to me, while I was praying earnestly on the subject, December 25th, 1832. (D&C 130:12–13)

The facts about the beginning of the U.S. Civil War are a well-known matter of history, both that the conflict began in South Carolina and was mostly over the "slave question." The fact that Joseph Smith correctly predicted these events nearly thirty years before they happened is begrudgingly acknowledged by anti-Mormons. However, they maintain that Joseph was a false prophet because the Civil War failed to bring about the second coming of Christ! What the prophecy says is that these events will occur prior to the second coming—and they did. Anti-Mormons contend that Joseph meant that Christ would come immediately following the bloodshed. That is not what Joseph wrote, nor is it what he meant.

The most common "evidence" used to accuse Joseph Smith of false prophecy deals with the timing of forecasted events. As in all scripture, the Lord uses the phrases "soon to be," "not many days [or years] hence," "the hour is nigh," "in this generation," and so on, to indicate events in the future. In some cases the referenced events are a few seasons away; in others they are hundreds or even thousands of years into the future. Since it is the Lord speaking through Joseph Smith in those revelations, Joseph uses the same phraseology. Many of the prophecies received by Joseph Smith will yet come to pass "not many years hence," and the Lord will bring about his works in his own time, in his own way, and through his own prophets. He has done so through Prophet Joseph Smith.

Aside from the many nonscriptural journal writings, documented discourses, and recorded teachings, Joseph Smith received revelation and inspiration to bring forth over 850 pages of divine communication from God. (Compare that to Moses' 308 pages, Isaiah's 80 pages, or Matthew's 54 pages.)

You might misunderstand, choose to disagree with, or misinterpret the writings of Moses, Isaiah, or Matthew. You could even argue, as many have, about whether these men were the true authors of the books that bear their names. These judgments do not, however, detract from the tremendous spiritual legacy they left as a result of their witnesses of the majesty of God and his kingdom. In the final analysis, their writings *exist*; they are there for us to see and handle. Moreover, they agree with each other about the millennia of the Lord's dealings with his children, as do the Joseph Smith's prophecies. In fact, the Lord clarifies the writings of each of these ancient prophets in the revelations of Joseph.

Those who cast aside the prophecies received by Joseph Smith and deride him as an evil man do not know him. They are as the men of old who were lesser beings and proved it by stoning the prophets sent in the name of the Lord.

Brigham Young taught that Adam was God

Brigham Young was the prophet and leader of the Latter-day Saints for thirty years. He is recognized by all commentators as one of the most able and dynamic leaders in American history. While Brigham Young wrote little, he was one of the most discursive and lucid of men. His theological lectures were well attended and recorded in the shorthand of the day, providing interesting insights into his thinking and speaking style. Some 390 of Brother Brigham's speeches were recorded in the *Journal of Discourses*, which were privately published in Liverpool, England, by an early Church stenographer. It is from these recordings that the "Adam-God" charge is made. (While the *Journal of Discourses* is often referred to as a source of insight and learning, it is not considered official statements of LDS Church doctrine.)

Anti-Mormon writers enjoy quoting a statement made by Brigham Young in April 1852. During the discourse, Brigham Young denied that the Holy Ghost was the father of Jesus Christ and affirmed

that the Savior was begotten by God the Father.
Brother Young explained: "Our Father in Heaven
begat all the spirits that ever were, or ever will be,
upon this earth; and they were born spirits in the
eternal world. Then the Lord by His power and
wisdom organized the mortal tabernacle of man."[42]
So, every human being is directly descended from
God the Father. He also said in that sermon, "The
earth was organized by three distinct characters,
namely Elohim, Jehovah, and Michael [Adam]."[43]
Later in this same sermon, President Young added,
"Jesus, our elder brother, was begotten in the flesh
by the same character that was in the garden of
Eden, and who is our Father in Heaven."[44] It is this
last statement on which anti-Mormons focus, ignoring Brigham's previous statements and the context of the sermon.

Adam holds a high place among the children of
men, literally standing at the head of the human
race. God, our Heavenly Father, "walked and talked
with Adam" in the Garden of Eden (see Gen. 3:8).
President Young's comment is a reference to God,
the Eternal Father. John A. Widtsoe wrote:

> The perspective of years brings out the
> remarkable fact, that, though the enemies of
> the Latter-day Saints have had access, in
> printed form, to the hundreds of discourses
> of Brigham Young, only half a dozen state-
> ments have been useful to the calumniators
> of the founder of Utah. Of these, the sermon

of April 9, 1852, which has been quoted most frequently, presents no errors of fact or doctrine, if read understandingly and honestly.[45]

Any researcher seeking truth and clarification would consider the whole body of knowledge on a subject before making concrete conclusions. Those who claim that Mormons believe and teach that Adam is God only discredit themselves and their scholarship because it is clear, from his statements before and after the 1852 discourses, that Brigham Young knew very well the true nature of both God our Heavenly Father and Adam, the father of the human family.

Mormons are living another gospel (Gal. 1:6–9)

Enemies of the restored gospel often quote passages from Paul's epistle to the Galatians as evidence that Mormonism is really "another gospel" (Gal. 1:6). They quote Galatians 1:8, which says, "But though we, or an angel from heaven, preach any other gospel unto you than that which we have preached unto you, let him be accursed." But their assertion is given false credence because, as has been stated earlier in this book, the gospel of Jesus Christ, of which Paul preached, has been restored to the earth in its fulness and is found in the one true church, The Church of Jesus Christ of Latter-day Saints. The "other gospel" Paul spoke of was the gospel being polluted by the Jews (see Gal. 1:14).

Paul, as an appointed servant of Jesus Christ, was simply taking appropriate ecclesiastical action to prevent the deterioration of Christ's gospel principles. It was his responsibility to correct the members of the Church when they erred—and they often did. Since the practices introduced by Christ were foreign to their traditions, the saints needed constant direction from Christ and his chosen leaders. After Paul and the other apostles were killed, none was left to make such corrections, and people fell away from the teachings of Christ. Consequently, churches established their own doctrines—apart from the revelations of God. The gospel of Christ has been restored in our times, and the Lord has appointed new leaders to correct the Saints when they err.

It is interesting that those who use this scripture to establish their anti-Mormon position are, in reality, a part of those who are following a theology that has been altered from the original by the traditions and the "cunning craftiness" of men (Eph. 4:14). Indeed, it is they who are following "another gospel" apart from the one established by Christ himself and restored in these last days through a prophet of God.

Mormons do not recognize the Bible as scripture

The Book of Mormon witnesses to the truthfulness of both the Old and New Testaments, confirming the authenticity of these historical records.[46] Thus, Mormons believe the Holy Bible to be "the word of God *as far as it is translated correctly*" [PGP, Article of Faith 8, emphasis added]. It is inspired scripture and is a testament of Jesus Christ. However, it is not a perfect scripture. The Bible has been translated more times than any other book. Also, there is not one Bible, but many. Having undergone numerous interpretations throughout the centuries, these Bibles have had precious parts taken out, while other passages have been changed to meet the demands of the interpreters. To say that the Bible is imperfect is not an implication of dishonesty, but of obvious human limitations.

Furthermore, most people think of the Bible as one book, when, in fact, the Bible is a collection of books, letters, and remembrances that span recorded history. Scholars suggest that four versions of the Old Testament originally existed. These were written and then edited numerous times over a period of at least five hundred years. The first Old Testament canon (authorized version) of the Jews contained twenty-four books. Catholic and Protestant editions are similar to the Jewish canon, but these groups divided some of the books, increasing the number to thirty-nine. The Greek Orthodox Church's version is the same as the Catholic canon, except the Greek Orthodox have five additional books.[47]

The New Testament records the life of Jesus Christ and the development of the early church.

The modern New Testament canon contains twenty-seven books that are generally accepted by both Protestants and Roman Catholics. It was not always that way, however. Books have been added and removed by different groups and religious leaders almost since biblical times.[48]

The first English language Bible was published less than five hundred years ago. The popular King James Version was published in 1611; the Revised King James Version was produced in 1885. Since then, there has been a raft of English language Bible translations—each claiming to clarify and improve on earlier texts.[49]

An example of a precious truth lost during Bible translation but preserved in the Book of Mormon follows. The Bible says there is one faith and one baptism (see Eph. 4:5), but it never completely explains the phrase. For example, what is that faith? And how or by whom is that baptism to be performed? Consequently, confusions abound in churches who are left to exercise religion based on their own interpretations. Compare the simple and inspired words of the Savior to the Book of Mormon people on this vital subject:

> He gave unto them power to baptize. And he said unto them: On this wise shall ye baptize; and there shall be no disputations among you.
>
> Verily I say unto you, that whoso repenteth of his sins through your words, and de-

sireth to be baptized in my name, on this wise shall ye baptize them—Behold, ye shall go down and stand in the water, and in my name shall ye baptize them.

And now behold, these are the words which ye shall say, calling them by name, saying:

Having authority given me of Jesus Christ, I baptize you in the name of the Father, and of the Son, and of the Holy Ghost. Amen.

And then shall ye immerse them in the water, and come forth again out of the water. (BM, 3 Nephi 11:22–26)

Generally, the Church uses the King James Version of the Bible in worship and study. The grace and beauty of this Bible translation, in addition to its general acceptance and availability, make it the most read and beloved of Bible translations. Mormons also believe the Book of Mormon to be the word of God and believe it to be Another Testament of the Lord Jesus Christ. It is precisely because Latter-day Saints use the Bible differently than do the traditional Judeo-Christians (i.e., supplementing it with other scripture and modern revelations) that anti-Mormons make the above claim. Elder McConkie explains:

When the Bible is read under the guidance of the Spirit, and in harmony with the

many latter-day revelations which interpret
and make plain its more mysterious parts, it
becomes one of the most priceless volumes
known to man.[50]

Furthermore, Latter-day Saints are counseled by
their leaders that Bible study is fundamental to understanding the gospel of Christ. Church officials
have stated that "'The Church of Jesus Christ of
Latter-day Saints accepts the Holy Bible as essential
to faith and doctrine' and that the Church is committed to Bible reading and scholarship."[51]

Mormonism is not biblically valid

Consider the biblical descriptions of Christ's
church. It is clear from the Bible that Christ selected
and ordained twelve apostles to lead his church (see
Mark 3:14; Luke 9:1–2; John 15:16). It is also clear
that Christ's church would have prophets, apostles,
elders, teachers, evangelists, deacons, priests, and
high priests to lead its members, as recorded in
Paul's letter to the Ephesians (see Eph. 2:20; 4:11).
Specific authority to function in the administration
of the Church by the power of God is called
"priesthood." This priesthood is obtained through
ordination by one having such authority under direction from Christ (see Ex. 40:15; Luke 9:1; 2 Cor.
10:7–8; Heb. 5:4–6). If members of Christ's true
church fell sick, they would call for "the elders"
(i.e., priesthood holders) of the Church, who would

anoint them with oil and bless and heal them, according to God's will (see Acts 14:23; James 5:14–15).

Christ's church would send forth missionaries, two-by-two, to preach the gospel (see Mark 6:7; Luke 10:1; John 20:21). The true church would have a law of health (see Eph. 5:18; 1 Cor. 6:19–20; 9:25–27) and would teach about a premortal existence, or pre-earth life (see John 17:5; Eph. 1:4–5). God the Father would be recognized as having created the individual spirits of all people; thus, we would all be brothers and sisters, spiritually (see Mal. 2:10; Matt. 12:50; Heb. 12:9). Members of Christ's true church would be called "saints" (see Rom. 1:7) and would be tithe payers (see Mal. 3:8–10; Heb. 7:4–5).

In Christ's church, once an investigator is repentant, baptism by immersion is essential (see Matt. 3:16; Mark 1:5, 9–10; Acts 8:38),[52] as is receiving the gift of the Holy Ghost (see John 3:5; Acts 2:38). Higher priesthood authority is required to bestow the Holy Ghost than is required to baptize (see Mark 1:7–8; Luke 3:16; Acts 19:2–6; John 1:33), and persons performing these ordinances must be duly authorized priesthood holders (see Matt. 3:11; Luke 3:16). Christ's true church will teach and testify that the Holy Ghost will bear witness of the truthfulness of the Savior's plan, when it is presented. In this way, any child of God can know which of the many churches teaches the principles of the Savior (see John 16:13–14; 1 Cor. 12:4–12; Eph. 1:17).

Christ's church would provide the opportunity for salvation for all of God's children, not just for those who receive the gospel while living on the earth. The members of his church would baptize for the dead (see 1 Cor. 15:29) and would build temples. These temples would have unique and holy purposes (see Isa. 2:3; Mal. 3:1).

The above listed biblical references are but a small portion of those that describe the attributes and characteristics of Christ's true church; however, these scriptural references provide a profile, or a blueprint, of what one may expect in any church calling itself Christ's. So, which of all the churches in the world best fits this profile? The Church of Jesus Christ of Latter-day Saints is the only church on earth that fits the Bible's description of Christ's church.

Mormons are saved by works

Mormons believe in the saving influence of the atonement of Jesus Christ. In fact, salvation comes because of the Atonement. In a latter-day revelation through Joseph Smith, the Lord said:

> And this is the gospel, the glad tidings, which the voice out of the heavens bore record unto us—
> That he came into the world, even Jesus, to be crucified for the world, and to bear the sins of the world, and to sanctify the world, and to cleanse it from all unrighteousness;

That through him all might be saved whom the Father had put into his power and made by him. (D&C 76:40–42)

Lehi, an ancient American prophet whose messages are recorded in the Book of Mormon, added:

Wherefore, redemption cometh in and through the Holy Messiah; for he is full of grace and truth.

Behold, he offereth himself a sacrifice for sin, to answer the ends of the law, unto all those who have a broken heart and a contrite spirit; and unto none else can the ends of the law be answered.

Wherefore, how great the importance to make these things known unto the inhabitants of the earth, that they may know that there is no flesh that can dwell in the presence of God, save it be through the merits, and mercy, and grace of the Holy Messiah, who layeth down his life according to the flesh, and taketh it again by the power of the Spirit, that he may bring to pass the resurrection of the dead, being the first that should rise.

Wherefore, he is the firstfruits unto God, inasmuch as he shall make intercession for all the children of men; and they that believe in him shall be saved. (BM, 2 Nephi 2:6–9)

Mormons do not believe that all one must do to attain eternal salvation is confess Christ. We believe that we must confess Christ, do his works, and endure to the end in order to qualify for the grace that is so freely offered.

This latter-day doctrine of grace is best illustrated by an ancient prophet on the American continent who wrote in the Book of Mormon:

> For we labor diligently to write, to persuade our children, and also our brethren, to believe in Christ, and to be reconciled to God; for we know that it is by grace that we are saved, after all we can do. (BM, 2 Nephi 25:23)

Can there be any question about Joseph Smith's feelings and LDS doctrine about the relationship between grace and works? Latter-day Saints do not believe their works will qualify them for eternal reward, but rather they work to build the kingdom of God on the earth because of their love for the Savior and their recognition of His all-saving grace.

Mormons are prejudiced against blacks

The claim that the LDS Church and its members are prejudiced against black people or exclude blacks from membership or worship has been around for some time. However, a careful review of Church history to this day presents quite a different picture.

People of African descent have been members of the Church almost since its organization in 1830. Several blacks joined the Church when they were slaves and, after being freed, went west with the great pioneer exodus from Missouri to Utah.[53]

While black members of the Church were relatively few in number in the Church's early days, their membership number has grown vigorously in recent years. Since the LDS Church membership records do not identify race, it is impossible to accurately measure the growth of black membership; however, statistics on membership in areas where people are largely or exclusively of African descent demonstrate significant growth. The first black African stake (a geographical unit of approximately 2500 Church members) was organized in Nigeria in 1988.[54]

Until June 1978 male black members of the Church could not hold the priesthood, function in callings requiring priesthood authority, or participate in temple or priesthood ordinances. The reasons for this restriction have not been given. Several explanations have been speculated on, by those both in and out of the Church, but no explanations have been given officially by the Church leadership.[55] It was anticipated that this restriction from the priesthood would be rescinded by revelation at some future date. As early as 1857 Brigham Young said that the "time will come when they will have the privilege of all we have the privilege of and more."[56] In June 1978 President

Spencer W. Kimball, then the prophet of the Church, announced the revelation that all worthy males could hold the priesthood.

Since the Church's early days, blacks have been welcomed and fellowshipped in the Church. Aside from the restriction of priesthood, blacks have participated in the Church and gospel without any demarcation between blacks and whites. During the civil rights movement in the 1960s, Protestant churches in the United States, South Africa, and other parts of the world routinely separated blacks and whites for worship and fellowship. No such separation ever existed in The Church of Jesus Christ of Latter-day Saints.

Black Latter-day Saints enjoy opportunities in all phases of Church activity, including missionary work, quorum leadership, and so on. People of African descent are openly sought by LDS missionaries and encouraged to come unto Christ, via the waters of baptism, and to remain faithful, serving one another in a spirit of harmony and love.

Mormon youth are forced to serve missions

Service as an LDS missionary is considered a great privilege by those who request such an assignment. Most Mormon missionaries are young (between the ages of 19 and 23). Others serve after retirement. Typically, those who request to serve a mission have looked forward to the opportunity for many years and have prepared both materially and spiritually for the experience. Once their preparation is completed, a formal request to serve is made to Church leaders. Usually within a few weeks, they receive acceptance and an assignment to serve somewhere in the world for a period of eighteen to twenty-four months. Prospective missionaries do not select their mission locations, so much excitement accompanies the receipt of a "call" to serve the people of an assigned area.

LDS missionaries serve without financial remuneration. In fact, most pay their own expenses for their entire time of service. Member donations help those who are unable to pay their own expenses. In addition to active proselytizing work, missionaries do significant public service in their assigned areas working as volunteers in schools, hospitals, homes for the elderly or the disabled, and doing spontaneous acts of Christian service as they arise.

While there is a strong missionary tradition in most LDS families and much encouragement from Church leadership to prepare for and serve honorable missions, especially for young men, no one is forced to serve in this way.

What about *The God Makers*?

According to its authors, *The God Makers* is both a film and a book with essentially the same anti-Mormon purpose: "exposing and bringing to full knowledge the real doctrines of false prophets

and teachers of the Mormon Church" and doing a
"service to the Christian community by keeping
them informed, equipping them . . . that they may
be effective witnesses."[57] The film has high production values and is clearly not the work of amateurs.
The use of a highly skilled filmmaker is evident, as
is the high cost associated with a production of this
quality.

Both the film's and the book's contents, how-
ever, leave much to be desired in its supposedly
forthright service of "keeping [people] informed."
Rather than give my own views on this subject,
I've chosen several statements by prominent non-
Mormons who have seen the film or read the book.

In his book *The Truth about "The God Makers,"*
Gilbert Scharffs provides a 400-page exposé of *The
God Makers*'s lies, distortions, and deceptions. In
the introduction, Scharffs lists a subjective tabula-
tion (shown on opposite page) in an attempt to
classify the errors within *The God Makers* into
various categories. In all, there are well in excess of
six hundred errors in *The God Makers*. (See page 95
for more on *The God Makers*'s producers).

Rhonda M. Abrams, Regional Director of the
Anti-Defamation League of B'nai B'rith, makes the
following statement of her professional reaction to
the film:

> The use of a documentary format with a
> factual tone is a clever ploy to convey a high

Repetition of charges from once to several times	169
Statements that were not true	141
Unwarranted conclusions based on known facts	131
Misinterpreted statements	125
Exaggerated statements	119
Broad generalizations	48
Significant quotes or charges without documentation	47
Historical material quoted out of context which altered the meaning	39
Scriptures quoted out of context or paraphrased incorrectly which altered the meaning	18
Footnote references that were not where they were indicated	7
Wrong footnote because the source copied by the authors had the wrong footnote also	5

Figure 1. Scharffs's list of errors in *The God Makers*.

degree of believability to what is in fact merely an anti-Mormon work. I am fearful that many of those viewing "The Godmakers," especially those who are unfamiliar with the tenets of the Church of Latter Day Saints, will come away believing much of what they see.

Those who view it carefully, however, can see just how invidious and defamatory "The Godmakers" is.[58]

W. John Koystra of the Institute for Communal Christianity in Toronto, Canada, writing to Mr. Richard R. Robertson of Public Communications in Markham, Ontario, on 18 April 1990, made the following statement:

> Over Easter I have reviewed the videos *The God Makers* and *Temple of the God Makers* and have decided that we will not catalog these two films as part of our collection of Mormon reference materials. . . . I find these two films personally insulting and consider them a prime example of the unethical practices employed by so many of the evangelical churches and TV ministries. The decision not to include these was not an easy one, for I have a natural dislike for censorship, however in this case I must concur with Plato and conclude that their content is sufficiently dangerous so as to be potentially destructive of that which is good, while at the same time not making a significant contribution to a knowledge of Mormonism.

In an advisory report to religious executives in March–April 1984, the National Conference of Christians and Jews Inc. (NCCJ), made the following statement regarding *The God Makers*:

> Because showing of *The Godmakers* is an integral part of the program of the Concerned Christians group, we offer these opinions based on our viewing of the film, research and reflection.
>
> The film does not—in our opinion—fairly portray the Mormon Church, Mormon history, or Mormon belief. It makes extensive use of "half-truth," faulty generalizations, erroneous interpretations, and sensationalism. It is not reflective of the genuine spirit of the Mormon faith. . . .
>
> It appears to us to be a basically unfair and untruthful presentation of what Mormons really believe and practice.[59]

The Arizona Regional Board of the NCCJ wrote:

> We believe that most fair-minded people who would happen to view this film would be appalled by it, because their attitudes have been previously formed through many day-by-day experiences with Mormons which demonstrate that they are good friends, neighbors and fellow citizens.

There are, unfortunately, some who lack
adequate knowledge about the Mormon
faith, who may unwarily be misled by this
film. We recommend to all persons that they
utilize every opportunity for face-to-face dialogue with their neighbors in an atmosphere
of mutual respect.[60]

The God Makers is the closest thing to religious
pornography that can exist. In my opinion, its crea-
tors are not seeking to enlighten anyone, but wish
only to enrich themselves by appealing to the
prejudices and base instincts of those who promote
and buy their wares.

Unanswered questions and charges

In any endeavor there are unanswered questions—
or at least answers that do not entirely satisfy the
questioner. An example might be: Why, in the New
Testament, did the accounts of Mark and Luke
differ regarding the visit of the women to the open
and empty sepulchre? Mark says there was only one
angel in the tomb; Luke says there were two.
Moreover, the reported conversations between the
women and the heavenly beings are different in
each account. Which account is right? For me, it
really does not matter. The important point is that
an angel or angels were there and that Christ was
resurrected and lives today. I could—and some
do—disbelieve the Bible because of such apparent

contradictions. Such a deduction is tragic because it keeps the evaluator from receiving eternal blessings and needed comfort from the inspired and pure teachings of the Holy Bible.

There are teachings in the Bible that can be stumbling blocks to those seeking a purely intellectual witness. These same stumbling blocks exist for those who dwell on obscure and seemingly unexplainable points of Church history; the lives of Adam, Noah, Jacob, or Joseph Smith; and the Book of Mormon. For example, at one point in his ministry, Jesus Christ taught the basic principles of the sacrament—the symbolic eating of the flesh and blood of the Savior in remembrance of the covenants made to follow him and to keep his commandments. For some reason this was a hard doctrine for the disciples to understand and follow, probably because it was new and different from their traditions. At that point Christ's popularity was at its highest, but the scriptures say, "From that *time* many of his disciples went back, and walked no more with him" (John 6:66).

Christ's teachings in the meridian of time and also those revealed in latter days contain "hard" doctrines. Many such doctrines can only be understood or appreciated through an accumulation of knowledge over a period of time and by study, experimentation, fasting, and prayer—efforts many are sadly unwilling to make. Failing to make the effort for understanding and revelation has held many people from the restored gospel; thus, these "hard" doctrines and the unanswered questions or charges concerning them become stumbling blocks instead of spiritual building blocks as the Lord intended.

When questions are asked out of context or are trivial, the questioner does not want answers, he wants to confuse the learner and to frustrate the learned. Some anti-Mormon authors claim that when the Church does not respond to attacks or questioning, those attacks must be true, or at least have truth in them. This is not so. The Church does not debate many anti-Mormon claims because to do so would consume valuable time and energy better spent in informing people about the Church's beliefs. To accomplish this goal, it has established the Public Communications Department in Salt Lake City, Utah, to disseminate information about the Church and its beliefs about specific doctrines and practices.

Basic Anti-Mormon History

One of the major reasons for hostility against the LDS Church has been the Church's belief in modern revelation (see page 36). The theological foundation of the LDS Church rests on the claim by Joseph Smith that he received, in answer to humble prayer, visits from God the Father, Jesus Christ, and angels who instructed him to restore a dispensation of the gospel.

Those who opposed Joseph Smith and this restoration of Christ's gospel on theological grounds did so because of what they believed about the Bible. They believed that the Bible was the only word of God—that God had spoken, and he need speak no more. Hence, there was no need for a modern-day prophet or a Restoration.

These anti-Mormons' philosophy was and is that any theological teaching must conform to their interpretation of the Bible, and that any teaching not fitting their exact rendering of biblical thought must necessarily be rejected—much like the Pharisees and Sadducees in the meridian of time rejected Jesus Christ as the Savior because he failed to live up to their preconceived ideas of the promised Messiah. This concept of doctrines having to conform to myopic interpretations of Bible teachings exists today and forms the basis for much anti-Mormon activity directed from sectarian clergy.

Skepticism about Joseph Smith and his testimony that he'd had a vision was understandable. At the time of Joseph's vision there was much religious excitement in American and many were claiming new ideas and even visions from God. However, Joseph had not only claimed communication from God and Jesus Christ, but he had produced the Book of Mormon as well, which was evidence of his sacred experiences. Those who opposed the Prophet found Joseph's testimony of receiving this book of "golden" plates—from an angel!—an astonishing claim; however, the book *existed* and had to be explained in some way. Accordingly, the first anti-Mormon activity was to try to explain away the Book of Mormon and to discredit Joseph and other early Church leaders.

The founder of the Disciples of Christ Church, Alexander Campbell, wrote the first published anti-Mormon pamphlet in 1832. In that pamphlet Campbell concluded: "I cannot doubt for a single minute that [Joseph Smith] is the sole author and proprietor of [the Book of Mormon]." Two years later he withdrew that statement and accepted the newly proposed theory that Joseph Smith had somehow collaborated with Sidney Rigdon, an early Church leader, to produce the Book of Mormon from a lost manuscript written by Reverend Solomon Spaulding (see page 43), a theory asserted by Eber D. Howe in his book *Mormonism Unvailed* [sic]. Howe's information came from "Doctor" Philastus Hurlbut, who was twice excommunicated from the Church for immorality. (Hurlbut was also hired by an anti-Mormon committee to find those who would attest to Joseph Smith's "dishonesty.") Hurlbut's research and ill-gotten affidavits produced much of the libelous history of the Smith family and of the early Church that is referenced by anti-Mormon writers today.[61]

Later, when Hurlbut and Howe finally located Spaulding's manuscript, they discovered that it had no demonstrable connection with the Book of Mormon. However, Howe's book still formed the basis for much of the anti-Mormon writing of the nineteenth and twentieth centuries.

I. Woodbridge Riley claimed, in his 1903 book *The Founder of Mormonism,* that Joseph Smith was an epileptic. Riley was also the first to suggest that the books *View of the Hebrews* (Ethan Smith) and *The Wonders of Nature and Providence Displayed* (Josiah Priest) were the sources of the Book of Mormon. In 1930 American historian Bernard De Voto asserted, in the *American Mercury,* that "unquestionably, Joseph Smith was a paranoid." (He admitted later that the article was a "dishonest attack.") In 1931 Harry M. Beardsley, in *Joseph Smith and His Mormon Empire,* published in 1931, asserted that Joseph's revelations, visions, and the Book of Mormon itself were simply by-products of Joseph's subconscious.

Fawn Brodie, in her 1945 book *No Man Knows My History,* portrayed Joseph Smith as a "myth-maker" who absorbed his theological ideas from his

rural New York environment. Brodie repudiated
the Spaulding theory and revived the original
Alexander Campbell thesis that Joseph Smith alone
was the author of the Book of Mormon. Then, in
1980 a book entitled *Who Really Wrote the Book of
Mormon?* was published by three anti-Mormons
who asserted that the Book of Mormon has its roots
in a second Spaulding manuscript that no one has
produced. Hence, after 160 years, anti-Mormon
writers have come back to where they started, with
nothing to show for the journey.[62]

Why Do Anti-Mormons
Do What They Do?

I believe a few anti-Mormons are simply misled. Like Paul before his conversion on the road to Damascus, they have a sincere desire to counter what they feel is wrong. Most of these people have not investigated the Church from within to any great extent but are hearkening the pronouncements of anti-Mormon writers and misdirected theologians. As was the case in Joseph Smith's day, many providers of anti-Mormon material are pastors or ministers of their own churches. These theologians have been trained to preach their own forms of Christianity—and also to fight against any church that fails to conform.

Another factor may be the unwritten creed between sectarian ministers: one pastor or minister does not proselytize from the congregation of another. Since LDS members and missionaries carry the message of the restored gospel to *all* who will listen, they are thereby breaking the creed and are thus open to attack.

While there are many church leaders who are sincerely and truly interested in the salvation of their followers, some are not. These church leaders are paid for the work they do. To them, being a minister is a career choice, above all else. The amount of payment received by them is usually de-

cided by a governing board and is obviously influenced by the amount of contributions made by their
congregations. Since The Church of Jesus Christ of
Latter-day Saints has no paid ministry and since the
Church is growing at a sustained rate through its
missionary efforts, it might represent a threat to the
financial well-being of sectarian church leaders.

There are also small groups of people who were
once members of the Church but fell away for various reasons or were excommunicated for actions
contrary to Church standards. Perhaps these people
were hurt or offended by someone in the Church or
by some disciplinary procedure and felt it necessary
for them to strike back militantly. Church leadership and membership could possibly learn from
these people how to be better leaders.

Further, I believe many anti-Mormons are
openly opposed to the Church because to actively
fight against it satisfies their desire for a sense of
power. Some have built up organizations that
openly persecute the Church and its representatives
by filling their adherents with recycled anti-Mormon dogma that fuels the effort.

Greed is an obvious factor. I find it interesting
that anti-Mormon books carry such a heavy price.
Having been associated with the printing business
for some time, I have a good idea of how much it
costs to publish a small, paperbacked book. You can
purchase most of these anti-Mormon books from
your local "Christian" bookstore *for ten to fifteen
dollars each*! In short, most anti-Mormon writers

do what they do because they make money at it. When they cannot locate enough material to satisfy their audiences, they recycle incorrect information or make up something new. There is a market for anti-Mormon literature, especially among the embittered, and where there is a market, someone will fill the demand. There was once a market for information concerning the whereabouts of Jesus Christ. For thirty pieces of silver, Judas Iscariot filled the demand.

Consider that Mormon missionaries give of themselves, their time, talents, and means, to serve the Savior wherever they are called. The message they bring is free of any charge or obligation. Copies of the Book of Mormon and other materials that explain the principles of the restored gospel are available free of cost to any person who is interested.

I conclude that those who write, sell, or promote the distribution of anti-Mormon materials are either grossly misled or openly deceitful. These are the modern-day equivalents of those who stoned the prophets and crucified the Lord.

Final Statement

The Church of Jesus Christ of Latter-day Saints is the church established by Jesus Christ himself, following the pattern he has always used—that is, revelation and leadership through prophets and apostles. The fulness of the gospel of Jesus Christ is contained in the doctrines and ordinances of his Church. Continuing revelations from God the Eternal Father are given to his appointed servant on the earth today—the president and prophet of the Church.

The Book of Mormon is the word of God recorded by ancient prophets on the American continent for the people of this day as a guide and a divine direction for their lives. This book truly is "a marvelous work and a wonder" (BM, 2 Nephi 25:17; 27:26) that gives meaning and clarity to the gospel of Jesus Christ. I know that the Book of Mormon is a true book of scripture and is a companion volume to the Holy Bible. Each child of God can receive his or her own personal witness of its truthfulness by following the promise of Moroni found in the Book of Mormon in Moroni 10:3–4. He outlines the sure way to gain a testimony of the true church of Jesus Christ.

I am a person of common emotions. I love my wife and children beyond my ability to express. The love I have for them gives me the strength to make

whatever sacrifice is necessary for their well-being.
Like any responsible father, I want the best for
them—not just "until death do us part," but for all
time and eternity. I acknowledge and witness that
God, our Heavenly Father, lives. His Son Jesus
Christ made it possible, by his infinite atonement,
for me to enjoy happiness in this life and to hope
for an eternity with my loved ones.

Since 1971 I have been an active member of The
Church of Jesus Christ of Latter-day Saints. I know
it is the true church of Jesus Christ upon the earth.
The authority to administer in the holy ordinances
has been restored in our day, that each person may
qualify for eternal blessings by obedience to the
teachings of the Savior. As a worthy priesthood
holder, I can bless my wife and my children.
Through the gift of the Holy Ghost bestowed upon
them at their baptisms, they can be directed all their
lives by sacred whisperings that will never invite to
do evil, but only to do good and to serve their
fellow beings, and thus be in the service of their
Father in Heaven.

Knowing what I know, I can confidently teach
my children important principles of life. I can be a
guide to them as they face real moral and ethical
issues on which the world is confused and frustrated. I can counsel them to spend their lives
learning everything they can about the gospel of
Jesus Christ as it was taught anciently and as it has
been restored through a prophet of God in our day.
I can also encourage them to learn as much as they

like about any other truth, knowing that by so doing they can only increase in their love of the Savior by what they learn. The truth anciently is the truth today and will ever be.

These blessings and countless others are available to all people on condition of their faith in the Lord Jesus Christ, sincere repentance for transgressions, baptism by immersion by one having authority, and receiving the gift of the Holy Ghost by the laying on of hands. This is the "strait and narrow path" (BM, 2 Nephi 31:18–20) leading back to a glorious reunion with our God and with our families in the eternal kingdom of heaven.

There are many who would block the way, many who would create a dense fog, that we might lose our way and fall by the wayside. Some will counsel that we cannot depend on spiritual promptings because the Lord will not speak to us in this day. Those who teach such doctrines would mislead and keep others from eternal blessings.

Listen to the voice and spirit of the Lord Jesus Christ within you as you proceed in your personal quest for truth, and ponder the words of the Savior:

> Wherefore, my beloved brethren, I beseech of you in words of soberness that ye would repent, and come with full purpose of heart, and cleave unto God as he cleaveth unto you. And while his arm of mercy is extended towards you in the light of the day, harden not your hearts. . . .

For behold, after ye have been nourished by the good word of God all the day long, will ye bring forth evil fruit, that ye must be hewn down and cast into the fire?

Behold, will ye reject these words? Will ye reject the words of the prophets; and will ye reject all the words which have been spoken concerning Christ, after so many have spoken concerning him; and deny the good word of Christ, and the power of God, and the gift of the Holy Ghost, and quench the Holy Spirit, and make a mock of the great plan of redemption, which hath been laid for you?

Know ye not that if ye will do these things, that the power of the redemption and the resurrection, which is in Christ, will bring you to stand with shame and awful guilt before the bar of God?

And according to the power of justice, for justice cannot be denied, ye must go away into that lake of fire and brimstone, whose flames are unquenchable, and whose smoke ascendeth up forever and ever, which lake of fire and brimstone is endless torment.

O then, my beloved brethren, repent ye, and enter in at the strait gate, and continue in the way which is narrow, until ye shall obtain eternal life.

O be wise; what can I say more? (BM, Jacob 6:5–12)

Appendix: The Great Deceivers

The list of people who have challenged the origins, founders, or growth of The Church of Jesus Christ of Latter-day Saints is long indeed. Many anti-Mormon tracts and booklets are one-time publications with outrageous claims. They are often crudely done are usually distributed by hand. Other anti-Mormon publications have a professional appearance; they are published by large printing houses and are written by "experts" in comparative religion or by theologians whose academic credentials are clearly stated on the covers of their books in an attempt at credibility. To many, the development and distribution of anti-Mormon material is simply a commercial venture bringing millions of dollars to those who write, distribute, and sell this libelous literature.

In this section you will find a short synopsis of a few of the most prolific anti-Mormon writers, lecturers, and other "experts" on Mormonism. I have waded through most of their books and sat through many of their lectures and radio talk shows. In doing so I've found there is one thread of continuity that runs through their expressions: they lie. They sometimes openly lie, misquoting or fabricating statistics. Other times they slant their material in such a way that good appears as bad and bad as good.

Documentation relative to the claims made in this section is extensive and readily available. Also, while anti-Mormon writers commonly get away with extreme exaggeration and deception that cannot be proven or substantiated in any way, the information on the writers catalogued here is sure, available, and defensible.

Eber D. Howe and "Doctor" Philastus Hurlbut

The most notable anti-Mormon book written in the early days of the Church was *Mormonism Unvailed* [sic], published in 1834 by Eber D. Howe. Howe was a newspaper editor and printer in Painesville, Ohio, who published anti-Mormon writings, among other things.[63] *Mormonism Unvailed* was largely produced from a manuscript originally written by "Doctor" Philastus Hurlbut; however, Hurlbut's reputation was so bad that even those who were anxious for his book to be published were not eager to have Hurlbut's name associated with it. (Hurlbut was once a Methodist but was excluded for immoralities; then he joined the LDS Church but was excommunicated for immorality. Incidentally, Hurlbut's title of "doctor" came from his being the seventh son in his family not from a legitimate, qualifying education. In American folklore such titles were commonly given because of a superstition that the seventh son would possess supernatural qualities.)

Hurlbut was advised to sell the manuscript to Howe, which he did. Howe and Hurlbut were the first to assert that the Book of Mormon was a rewrite of a Solomon Spaulding manuscript allegedly obtained by early Church leader Sidney Rigdon. Later, when the Spaulding papers were located and researched, they were found to contain no correlation with the Book of Mormon. The two men then concocted the theory that Sidney Rigdon had written the Book of Mormon using another Spaulding manuscript.

One of Hurlbut's contributions consisted of obtaining affidavits from contemporaries of Joseph Smith who were willing to speak against the prophet or lend support to the Solomon Spaulding/Book of Mormon connection. Hurlbut provided both in significant numbers. It is interesting to note that the letters Hurlbut produced in support of the Spaulding/Book of Mormon connection contained no signatures from the authors or from any authenticator, and all were written in the same style! (Research into census records has shown that some of those attesting in the affidavits to specific conversations and observations were not even in the same state at the time of the alleged events!) It is probable that Hurlbut, eager to discredit Joseph Smith and Mormonism by any means, simply wrote these affidavits himself.

The flawed works of Hurlbut and Howe cast a rather long shadow in anti-Mormon history. In a previously referred to book entitled *Who Really*

Wrote the Book of Mormon?[64] the authors produce an unsigned letter from Spaulding's widow, Mrs. Solomon Spaulding Davison. The letter was published in the *Boston Recorder* in 1839. In this letter Mrs. Spaulding tells a long story about how she and her husband met, about early sicknesses and problems, and about how her husband wrote a historical romance, which she is sure is the foundation of the Book of Mormon. Sidney Rigdon, a former Disciple of Christ minister and an early LDS Church leader who had substantial religious training, had "ample opportunity . . . to copy it if he chose,"[65] she says. Further, in this letter she states: "Thus, a historical romance, with the addition of a few pious expressions and extracts from the sacred scriptures, has been constructed into a new Bible, and palmed off upon a company of poor deluded fanatics as divine."[66] It's a very compelling letter!

So eager to publish and broadcast such a juicy piece of "history," anti-Mormon writers failed to disclose an article from the Quincy, Illinois, *Whig* that appeared shortly after the *Boston Recorder* article. The *Whig* article exposes the Davison letter as a fabrication of D. Austin, of Monson, Massachusetts. Mr. Austin interviewed Mrs. Spaulding Davison, then he wrote the letter the way *he* wanted it written! In a subsequent interview with the former Mrs. Spaulding, the interviewer asked, "Did you, Mrs. Davison, write a letter to John Storrs, giving an account of the origin of the Book of Mormon?" She replied, "I did not." "Did you sign your name to it?" the gentleman asked. Mrs. Davison responded, "I did not, neither did I ever see the letter until I saw it in the *Boston Recorder*, the letter was never brought to me to sign."[67]

Peeling another layer off this anti-Mormon onion reveals other interesting information. Mrs. Spaulding states that Mr. Hurlbut took her husband's manuscript from her. He told her he would have it printed and give her "one half of the profits."[68] Later, he wrote to her and told her the manuscript would not be printed. Why? Solomon Spaulding explains, "I received a letter stating that it did not read as he expected, and he should not print it."[69] Clearly, the manuscript did not prove to be the origin of the Book of Mormon after all; therefore, it had little commercial value to Hurlbut. In a sworn affidavit by D. P. Hurlbut on 10 January 1881, he states:

> In the year [1834] . . . I went from Geauga County, Ohio, to Munson, Hampden County, Massachusetts, where I found Mrs. Davison, late widow of the Rev. Solomon Spaulding, late of Conneaut, Ashtabula County, Ohio. Of her I obtained a manuscript, supposing it to be the manuscript of the romance written by the said Solomon Spaulding, called the "Manuscript Found," which was reported to be the foundation of the "Book of Mormon." I did not examine the manuscript until I got home, when upon examination I found it to

contain nothing of the kind, but being a
manuscript upon an entirely different subject. This manuscript I left with E. D. Howe
. . . with the understanding that when he had
examined it, he should return it to the
widow.[70]

Hurlbut became an anti-Mormon when he was
rejected by the Church because of his repeated im-
moral actions. A proud man, "Doctor" Hurlbut did
everything in his power to refute the Church and
its founder. His clear motive was to make money
from his "inside information" about the Church.

He did make some money from the sale of the
book. From his gains he purchased a farm in the
township of Girard, Pennsylvania, and married.
Once, having been suspected of stealing, Hurlbut
fled the country to escape justice and was never
heard from again. By that time, the Hurlbut manuscript had long before become the adopted offspring
of Mr. E. D. Howe, whose name appears on the
cover.

Walter Ralston Martin

"Doctor" Walter R. Martin was the founder and
director of the Christian Research Institute in San
Juan Capistrano, California. His books *The Maze of
Mormonism* and *The Kingdom of the Cults* have
been common sources for the sectarian world to
turn to when seeking knowledge about The Church

of Jesus Christ of Latter-day Saints. Martin's books appear well documented, and his style of writing was bombastic in exposing the "serious threat" of the Mormon Church to Christian society, making very entertaining and compelling reading until you go beneath the surface and investigate his claims and credentials. Here's a sample:

Phony Academic Credentials

"Doctor" Walter Martin's only doctorate was from a nonaccredited correspondence school in Southern California, one step above a degree mill. He also claimed a master's degree in Comparative Religion. However, for years prior to getting his "doctorate," Walter Martin was referring to himself as "Doctor." On both of his most popular books, Martin claimed to have four degrees. His "degrees" are from Stony Brook School (a high school!), Adelphi University (where he attended for one semester), Biblical Seminary of New York (where he attended a summer session), and New York University (where he received a master's degree in Philosophy, not Comparative Religion, as he claimed).

In short, "Doctor" Martin did not hold a valid doctorate in anything.

False Ministerial Credentials.

Walter Martin commonly claimed to be an ordained Baptist minister of the Southern Baptist Convention and the American Baptist Convention.

However, Martin's only valid ordination was re-
voked in 1953. Yet, in a 1973 court document relat-
ing to his second divorce, Martin claimed, under
oath, to be "an ordained Minister of the American
Baptist Convention in good standing."[71] In a letter
from the Executive Director of the American Baptist Churches, USA, Reverend Linda C. Spoolstra
stated: "Walter Ralston Martin is not listed in the
American Baptist Churches' Professional Registry,
nor is he listed in our Directory of Professional
Church Leaders. This means that he has no standing in our denomination."[72] In a letter from the
Southern Baptist Agency, Barbara Denman wrote:
"We have searched our ... personnel records for
the name of Walter Martin, but are unable to come
up with anything. Evidently, he is not Southern
Baptist, nor is he ordained."[73]

Walter Martin's False Genealogy.

Walter Martin repeatedly claimed in his books,
in his lectures, and on radio shows that he was a
descendant of early Mormon leader Brigham
Young. In a taped lecture in 1977, he made this
statement to his audience:

> Wayne Cowdrey and I are very close be-
> cause he is a descendant of Oliver Cowdery,
> who allegedly wrote down the Book of
> Mormon that Joseph dictated. He is now a
> reborn Christian. I am a descendant of
> Brigham Young—successor to Joseph Smith,

ruler of the Latter-day Saints Church—a born again Christian.

Walter Martin was not a descendant of Brigham Young. That was proven in a public setting in 1984, whereupon Martin changed his claim.[74] He then said he was related to one of Brigham's brothers—also a false claim. (As it turns out, Wayne Cowdrey was not a descendant of Oliver Cowdery either—note the surname spellings. Oliver Cowdery's only surviving child, a daughter, died childless!)

Martin's "Sloppy Scholarship."
Martin claimed to be an authority on the doctrines and the finances of the LDS Church. In the preface of his book *The Maze of Mormonism,* he stated: "The facts herein contained must be sound and reliable if the conclusions arrived at are to be considered valid. . . . [I] have made every effort to accomplish this goal of accuracy."[75]

However, inside the text of his book, Martin proves to be pathetically inaccurate on every issue. For example, on pages 16–22 he illustrates "the Mormon threat," claiming that Mormons own or control major businesses in the U.S. and have enormous wealth and holdings to create a position of power. Research into his claims has proven him wrong![76] Martin depended on the sensationalism of his claims to carry the day for him. The information he lied about is readily available from the public corporations involved or from widely published industry statistics. Martin clearly assumed that his adherents would not check his references or dispute his conclusions.

Martin's Christian Research Institute (CRI), once a small rented suite in a modest business complex, showed $12,000,000 in gross income from 1979 to 1982, and as a "religious" organization, CRI paid no taxes. Thus, it is a well-funded, growing institution benefiting Martin's pocketbook. Further, in a 1985 *Newsweek* article, Martin's book *The Kingdom of the Cults* was listed among the most popular religious books of the day. At that point it had sold 319,350 copies at $14.95—that's $4,774,282 in gross income. Obviously, Martin's attack on the Church has been profitable for him.

J. Edward Decker

Ed Decker, a former Mormon, is the founder of an organization in Issaquah, Washington, named Saints Alive in Jesus Christ, or Ex-Mormons for Jesus, a group of "reformed" Mormons.[77]

Decker has written a few crude pamphlets about the LDS Church that make sensational statements about Mormonism, Church leaders, doctrines, and so on, but his most infamous works are the film productions *The God Makers, Temple of the God Makers,* and *The God Makers II.* In these documentary-style films (also available in written format), Decker and cohort Richard Baer claim to "reveal" the so-called evil empire of the LDS Church to the

curious or the unknowing. Decker has stated publicly that controversy and dispute are a part of his
nature. The major themes of *The God Makers* films
are (1) that the LDS Church's strong family image is
false and that the Church actually destroys families
and promotes divorce; (2) that the Church is a pow-
erful non-Christian cult that teaches and practices
blasphemy and performs occult rituals; and (3) that
members work their way to godhood while neglect-
ing Jesus Christ and worshipping Joseph Smith.

Decker must have done well on *The God Makers* because he followed it with a sequel, *The God
Makers II*. This second version is just as evil and
false as the first, representing religious bigotry at its
worst. In *The God Makers II* Decker attacks Church
leaders, making groundless accusations of sexual
immorality. This is an old claim that has been
proven by independent legal counsel to be without
any basis in fact. Decker then accused the Church of
another warmed-over charge—misuse of Church
funds. Again, this charge has been completely refuted. *The Arizona Republic,* the major newspaper
in Arizona, sent in a team of reporters to investigate Church finances and ultimately concluded that
such finances were managed honestly and judi-
ciously.

Then Decker moved on to "expose" the Church
as a seedbed of Satanic worship and child abuse!
Again, Decker's claims have been refuted. The
Church has aggressively and publicly addressed
both issues in all of society, promoting enforcement

of law for perpetrators, and understanding and support for victims.

Finally, Decker took on the Brigham Young University Jerusalem Center, saying it is being used as a center for proselytizing against a carefully worked out relationship with the State of Israel. Once again, Decker is wrong on all counts. Both the conditions of the BYU Jerusalem Center and the trusting and amiable relationship with the city of Jerusalem are well intact.

While Decker's deception is clear to those who know the truth, those without the benefit of either knowledge of LDS Church policies, teachings, and doctrines or without experience in the Church could be negatively influenced by his lies. And lie he does. Extensive studies have been made into Decker's claims, revealing his lies and deception.[78]

Decker has made public statements that he is not in it for the money. One could question that claim. Thousands of his videotapes have been purchased by various Protestant churches at $85 per videotape. His books are bestsellers among a certain population of evangelical Christians. Ed Decker is doing quite well as a champion of born-again believers. He has answers for everything, but he does not allow any questions!

Dee Jay Nelson

While Dee Jay Nelson never wrote an anti-Mormon book, his fame as an expert on Latter-day

scripture is far reaching. Nelson is quoted in numerous anti-Mormon works, including books by
Walter Martin, Wayne L. Cowdrey, and Jerald and
Sandra Tanner, to name a very few. An investigation into Dee Jay Nelson's claims is a fascinating
journey into almost unbelievable deception. Nelson's lies were so inventive and preposterous that
he provides a "high-water mark" for deception and
falsehood in anti-Mormon activity.

Nelson's primary activity and livelihood for
twelve years was giving anti-Mormon lectures to
various Christian churches. He primarily focused
on the book of Abraham, a book of ancient scripture
written on papyri and discovered in 1831 with the
remains of an Egyptian mummy. These papyri were
translated by Joseph Smith and are a part of the
latter-day scripture known as the Pearl of Great
Price.

Nelson alleged that Joseph Smith's translation
of the papyri was incorrect, which allegedly proved
that Joseph was not a prophet of God. He also
claimed that the LDS Church asked him to study
and translate the book of Abraham in the Joseph
Smith Papyri and agreed to publish his works. (See
page 47 for more on this claim.) But the fabric of
Dee Jay Nelson's claims and assertions breaks down
quickly when exposed.

"Professor" Dee Jay Nelson was never a professor, doctor (Ph.D.), or renowned Egyptologist. Nelson was a high school and college dropout who
forged his credentials or bought them from a degree

mill in Seattle, Washington (Pacific Northwestern University).[79] He claimed to have been employed by King Farouk, the last monarch of Egypt, and that King Farouk was so impressed with his work that he awarded him "a small collection of Egyptian antiquities."[80] Nelson also claimed to have been asked by the Egyptian government to calculate the weight of the inner coffin of Tutankhamen.

Dr. El Zeini, an Egyptologist living in Cairo who was closely associated with the Cairo Museum, was asked about Dee Jay Nelson and his connection to the Museum and to King Farouk. Zeini replied, "It is a well-established fact that the late King Farouk was an astute collector. It is quite impossible to think that he would consult a free-lance Egyptologist or confide in him his voluminous collection when he could have at hand the expert advise [sic] of the top notch Egyptologists of the time."[81] In the same letter, Zeini writes, "I have inquired from all the veteran Egyptologists who were working in the Antiquities Department in Egypt about the identity of Mr. D. J. Nelson. No one seems to remember this name or to recollect having seen him participate in any known excavation."[82]

Was Nelson asked by the Egyptian Government to calculate the weight of the inner coffin of Tutankhamen? No. The Egyptian government did not ask anyone to calculate it in Nelson's time because the calculation had already been done! Further, Nelson's calculation was a grossly inaccurate one copied from an error in a previous publication.[83]

In his lecture in Mesa, Arizona, on 22 February 1980, Dee Jay Nelson said:

> Now, before I begin the lecture, I want to say something about my credentials. Since I have been in the Valley, there has been much said against me in that respect. . . . You can check my credentials. I make my living as an Egyptologist. I'm paid for it. I'm either an Egyptologist or I'm fooling a lot of people . . . Well, I think that will be enough on that topic, but if you doubt that I have my degree, and my degree is in Anthropology, not Egyptology, you remember then, write these people that I mentioned and you will find out the truth of the matter!

Robert L. and Rosemary Brown of Mesa, Arizona, took Nelson's challenge and put him out of business. The couple completed a wonderful exposé of Dee Jay Nelson in their book *They Lie in Wait To Deceive*, vol. 1. The information they unearthed in their extensive research unravels a story of deception that taxes the imagination. Once Dee Jay Nelson was exposed, his professional influence was completely removed from him. He was no longer in demand as a lecturer or as an expert on Mormon scripture.[84] Dee Jay Nelson's works, however, live on in the spurious publications that continue to tout his wisdom, experiences, and credentials.

Jerald and Sandra Tanner

The Tanners are hailed by enemies of the LDS Church as scholars and as truthseekers. In the film *The God Makers,* they are introduced as former Mormons who have established an international reputation for their supposedly accurate and thorough research. Their attack on the Church has mostly focused on differences between various historical accounts of early LDS Church events and on changes to LDS scriptures. Their first published book, *The Changing World of Mormonism,* is virtually contained in their later, more exhaustive publication *Mormonism—Shadow or Reality?* which has been reprinted and widely distributed. This latter work is nearly six hundred pages long and requires a formidable effort just to wade through it. It would appear that the Tanners' tactic is to throw everything but the "kitchen sink" at the subject in the hopes of prevailing by sheer volume.

Those who take the time to read *Mormonism— Shadow or Reality?* (as I have) will find that the bulk of the material contributing to the volume is simply the same information repeated over and over in different sections of the book. Much of the Tanners' argument would not be an argument at all if it weren't for the creative conclusions they put forth and for the imaginative—and unethical—way

they extract material from LDS history and scripture. In the preface to *Mormonism—Shadow o r
Reality?* the Tanners write: "The fact that [the LDS
Church] would allow 65,000 copies to be published
without an official response seems to show that
there are no real answers to the questions we have
raised." Later in the same paragraph they add: "The
truth of the matter is that the Church leaders do not
mind controversy if they feel they can come out
ahead. We believe, however, that the Church has
too many secrets to hide to come out in open opposition to [this book]."

The truth of the matter is that LDS Church leadership will not officially comment on anti-Mormon
claims or arguments because expending Church re-
sources and energy in that way would detract from
the Church's objective to proclaim the gospel of
Jesus Christ. The Tanners repeatedly use this policy
to their advantage, sowing doubt in the hearts of
those who are unaware of the Church's policy.

To refute the truthfulness of the Tanners' product and the scholarship of their research, I will cite
one typical example. In the video *The God Makers*,
Sandra Tanner points to Mormon texts about the
Prophet Joseph Smith's first vision that appear con-
tradictory.[85] The point in question is, who, exactly,
appeared to the boy Joseph in the Sacred Grove? In
a section entitled "Source of Confusion" of *Mormonism—Shadow or Reality?* that deals with the
First Vision, the Tanners edit various statements by

early Church leaders to make them appear to say something they do not.

For example, the couple cite a quotation by early Church leader Heber C. Kimball that appears to confuse the account of Joseph's first vision. Breaking off with an ellipsis (. . .) at the beginning of the quotation, the authors interject comments and summarize Kimball's statement; then they return again to the quotation, making it appear a complete and connected thought. In reality, those two quotations were three paragraphs—237 words—apart in the referenced text! And the topic of the speech was not the First Vision, but Kimball was referring to a principle of divine delegation—an entirely different subject! Also, Kimball's reference was to an event that took place seven years after the First Vision. The Tanners lead their readers to believe otherwise. So much for truth and scholarship.

The example cited above represents a common practice of the Tanners. One Tanner critic, cited in an article entitled "Career Apostates," has said it best:

"Jerald and Sandra Tanner have read widely enough in the sources of LDS history to provide that [larger] perspective, but they do not. Although the most conscientious and honest researcher can overlook pertinent sources of information, the repeated omissions of evidence by the Tanners suggest an intentional avoidance of sources that modify or refute their caustic interpretation of Mormon history."[86]

A non-Mormon scholar (Lawrence Foster, associate professor of American history at the Georgia Institute of Technology) who has spent many years of intensive work on Mormonism and its history says this of the Tanners:

> The Tanners have repeatedly assumed a holier-than-thou stance, refusing to be fair in applying the same debate standard of absolute rectitude which they demand of Mormonism to their own actions, writings, and beliefs. . . .
> The Tanners seem to be playing a skillful shell game in which the premises for judgment are conveniently shifted so that the conclusion is always the same—negative.[87]

A close study of the arguments and tactics of Pharisees during the savior's earthly ministry shows a distinctively similar "shell game." Jerald and Sandra Tanner are career anti-Mormons—that is, slandering the Church is how they make their living. They have published numerous writings based on their "impeccably accurate" research and on the research of other associates, which even a nonscholarly review reveals as biased, misinterpreted, and imaginatively distorted.

Regarding anti-Mormons who oppose God's established church, The Church of Jesus Christ of Latter-day Saints, Bruce R. McConkie stated:

Everywhere—on every hand, among all sects, parties, and denominations; everywhere—among every nation, and kindred, and tongue, and people; everywhere—from one end of the earth to the other—everywhere those who hate and persecute the saints do it because they reject Christ. No matter that they may give lip service to his holy name; no matter that they think he is their God; no matter that they follow what they falsely suppose is his plan of salvation— they in fact are rejecting the living Christ when they reject and persecute those whom he hath called and sent forth to preach his word. And all of this is because, regardless of what false assumptions they may make as to their own forms of worship, they know not the One who sent Christ into the world.[88]

Endnotes

[1] Wayne L. Cowdrey, Howard A. Davis, and Donald R. Scales, *Who Really Wrote the Book of Mormon?* (Santa Ana, Calif.: Vision House, 1980).

[2] See James E. Talmage, *The Great Apostasy* (Salt Lake City, Utah: Deseret Book, 1978) and B. H. Roberts, *The Falling Away* (Salt Lake City, Utah: Deseret Book, 1950).

[3] For example, baptism by immersion was changed to baptism by sprinkling, baptism of infants was introduced, and Church organization was eventually altered to facilitate a "politically correct" theology.

[4] *World Book Encyclopedia*, 1988 ed., s.v. "Constantine the Great."

[5] Ibid., s.v. "Augustine."

[6] Ibid., s.v. "Reformation."

[7] Ibid., s.v. "Pentecostal churches."

[8] Ibid., s.v. "The United Church of Canada."

[9] John Cotton, *A Reply to Mr. Williams* . . . , ed. J. Lewis Diman, in *Complete Writings*, 2:14, 50, cited by Donald Skaggs, *Roger Williams' Dream for America* (New York: Peter Lang, 1993), 43.

[10] Skaggs, *Dream for America*, 49.

[11] Albert C. Outler, ed., "Sermon 89: The More Excellent Way," in *The Works of John Wesley, Sermons 71–114* (Nashville, Tenn.: Abingdon Press, 1986), 3:263–264.

[12] See also The Church of Jesus Christ of Latter-day Saints, *Church History in the Fulness of Times* (Salt Lake City, Utah: The Church of Jesus Christ of Latter-day Saints, 1989), 34.

[13] Spencer W. Kimball, "Absolute Truth," ENSIGN (September 1978): 3–8.

[14] See Joseph Smith, *Teachings of the Prophet Joseph Smith*, comp. Joseph Fielding Smith (Salt Lake City, Utah: Deseret Book, 1976), 324.

[15] Stephen E. Robinson, *Are Mormons Christians?* (Salt Lake City, Utah: Bookcraft, 1991), 91–92.

[16] Ibid., 92.

[17] Augustine, *Reply to Faustis*, 22.47, cited in Robinson, op. cit., 93.

[18] *World Book Encyclopedia*, 1988 ed., s.v. "cult."

[19] See Walter R. Martin, *Mormonism—The Modern Cult Library* (Grand Rapids, Mich.: Zondervan Publishing House, 1963), preface.

[20] *Webster's Third New International Dictionary*, s.v. "Christian."

[21] Bruce R. McConkie, *Mormon Doctrine* (Salt Lake City, Utah: Bookcraft, 1979), 129.

[22] For more information, see Robinson, *Are Mormons Christians?*

[23] LDS Article of Faith 1 (found in the PGP) states: "We believe in God, the Eternal Father, and in His Son, Jesus Christ, and in the Holy Ghost."

[24] McConkie, *Mormon Doctrine*, 319. See also Robinson, *Are Mormons Christian?* 71–89.

[25] *Teachings of the Prophet Joseph Smith*, 370–371.

[26] C. S. Lewis, *Mere Christianity* (New York: Macmillan, 1952), 174–175.

[27] *Teachings of the Prophet Joseph Smith*, 111.

[28] McConkie, *Mormon Doctrine*, 643.

[29] Ibid., 648.

[30] *Merriam Webster's Collegiate Dictionary*, 10th ed., s.v. "worship."

[31] McConkie, *Mormon Doctrine*, 849.

[32] See also D&C 59:5 and D&C 135.

[33] Gordon B. Hinckley, "Joseph the Seer," ENSIGN (May 1977): 65, cited by Daniel H. Ludlow, "A Tribute to Joseph Smith, Jr.," in *The Prophet Joseph: Essays on the Life and*

Mission of Joseph Smith, ed. Larry C. Porter and Susan Easton Black (Salt Lake City: Deseret Book, 1988), 334.

[34] Roger R. Keller, *The Mormons: Fact Versus Fiction* (Nashville, Tenn.: Scarritt Graduate School, 1986), 3.

[35] For example, at times Joseph talks about Jesus speaking to him but doesn't explicitly say that God was present as well. Anti-Mormons contend that this means Joseph contradicted himself about who appeared to him in the First Vision, which is nonsense.

[36] The book was Cowdrey, et al., *Who Really Wrote the Book of Mormon?*

[37] Robert J. Matthews, "Why Have Changes Been Made in the Printed Editions of the Book of Mormon?" in *A Sure Foundation* (Salt Lake City, Utah: Deseret Book, 1988), 35.

[38] Ibid., 34.

[39] See ENSIGN (Sept. 1976, pp. 77–82; Oct. 1981, pp. 8–19) and *BYU Studies* (Fall 1982, pp. 387–423) for more information on corrections in the 1981 edition of the Book of Mormon.

[40] For further information on changes made to the Book of Mormon, see Matthews, "Changes," 33–39.

[41] Robert A. Morey, *How to Answer a Mormon* (Minneapolis, Minn.: Bethany House Publishers, 1983), 17.

[42] George D. Watt, *Journal of Discourses* (Liverpool, England, 1855), 1:50.

[43] Ibid.

[44] Ibid., 51.

[45] John A. Widtsoe, *Evidences and Reconciliations,* collector's ed., arr. G. Homer Durham (Salt Lake City, Utah: Bookcraft, 1987), 71.

[46] Robert J. Matthews, "How Can I Explain the Church's Attitude toward the Bible?" in *A Sure Foundation,* 160.

[47] The Greek Orthodox canon's five additional books are 1 and 2 Esdras, Psalm 151, *The Prayer of Manasseh,* and *3 Maccabees.*

[48] In the first canon (prior to A.D. 200—Muratorian) the books of Hebrews, James, and 1 and 2 Peter were not considered

scripture, but the canon did include two other works, *The Apocalypse of Peter* and The Wisdom of Solomon. In about A.D. 300, the Christian church considered the books of Hebrews, James, Jude, and Revelation to be questionable and spurious. More than a thousand years later, Martin Luther did not consider these four books to be worthy to remain among the "true and noblest books of the New Testament" (see preface to Lutheran Bible)—he even went so far as to call James "a letter of straw"—and for a time, these books were removed from Luther's canon.

[49] These include the *Moffat Bible* (NT: 1913; OT: 1924), *The Bible: An American Translation* (1931), *Revised Standard Version* (NT: 1946; OT: 1952; AP: 1957), *The New English Bible* (NT: 1961; OT and AP: 1970), *New American Standard Bible* (NT: 1963; all: 1971), *The Good News Bible* (NT: 1966; OT: 1976), *The Jerusalem Bible* (1966), *The New American Bible* (1970), and *The Common Bible* (1973), to name a few.

[50] McConkie, *Mormon Doctrine*, 83.

[51] Daniel H. Ludlow, *Encyclopedia of Mormonism*, s.v. "Bible: First Presidency's endorsement of Bible reading."

[52] See also Rom. 6:3–5 and Col. 2:12 for symbolism of baptism in this manner.

[53] For examples of black pioneers and early Church members, see Newell G. Bringhurst, *Saints, Slaves, and Blacks: The Changing Place of Black People within Mormonism* (Westport, Conn.: Greenwood Publishing, 1981) and Kate B. Carter, *The Story of the Negro Pioneer* (Salt Lake City, Utah: Utah Printing, 1965), also published in *Our Pioneer Heritage* (Salt Lake City, Utah: Daughters of the Utah Pioneers, 1965), 8:497–580.

[54] "Stakes, Missions, Temples," *Church Almanac*, 1991–1992 ed. (Salt Lake City, Utah: Deseret News, 1990), 221, 224.

[55] It was generally maintained that blacks should be denied the priesthood because of their lineage. According to the book of Abraham, the descendants of Cain were to be denied the priesthood of God (PGP, Abraham 1:21–27).

[56] Brigham Young, "Brigham Young Papers," 5 February 1852, LDS Church Archives.

[57] Gilbert W. Scharffs, *The Truth about "The God Makers"* (Salt Lake City, Utah: Publishers Press, 1989), Appendix A, 382.

[58] Ibid., 379.

[59] Ibid., 383–384.

[60] Ibid., 384.

[61] See also Richard Lloyd Anderson, "Joseph Smith's New York Reputation Reappraised," *BYU Studies* 10 (Spring 1970): 283–314.

[62] Much of the information for this chapter was obtained from an article in Ludlow's *Encyclopedia of Mormonism*, s.v. "anti-Mormon publications," 45–52.

[63] Stanley B. Kimball, "The Anthon Transcript: People, Primary Sources, and Problems," *BYU Studies* , 10/3 (1970): 343.

[64] See Cowdrey, et al., *Who Really Wrote the Book of Mormon?* 42–6.

[65] Robert L. Brown and Rosemary Brown, *They Lie in Wait to Deceive*, revised ed. (Mesa, Ariz.: Brownsworth Publishing, 1986), 2:229.

[66] Ibid., 230.

[67] Ibid., 232.

[68] Ibid.

[69] Ibid.

[70] Ibid., 234.

[71] Brown and Brown, *They Lie in Wait to Deceive* (Mesa, Ariz.: Brownsworth Publishing, 1986), 3:8.

[72] Ibid., 9.

[73] Ibid., 17.

[74] Ibid., 69–91.

[75] Walter R. Martin, *The Maze of Mormonism* (Grand Rapids, Mich.: Zondervan Publishing House, 1962), 12.

[76] Brown and Brown, *They Lie in Wait to Deceive*, 3:135–178.

⁷⁷ I had firsthand experience with Decker and his followers when I lived in the Seattle area in 1975–76. They distributed their flyers by leaving them on cars parked in LDS meetinghouse parking lots.

⁷⁸ For more information about the falsity of Decker's claims, see Gilbert W. Scharffs, *The Truth about "The God Makers," Part II*; James A. Carver, *The New Mythmakers: A Reply to the Film "The God Makers"*; or Brown and Brown, *They Lie in Wait to Deceive*, vol. 4. Full references for these publications are in the bibliography at the end of this book.

⁷⁹ Pacific Northwestern University was shut down by the State of Washington Attorney General's office in 1980. See Brown, *They Lie in Wait to Deceive*, vol. 1 (Mesa, Ariz.: Brownsworth Publishing, 1981) for more information about Dee Jay Nelson's credentials.

⁸⁰ Brown and Brown, *They Lie in Wait to Deceive*, 1:97.

⁸¹ Ibid., 98.

⁸² Ibid.

⁸³ Ibid., 84.

⁸⁴ At the time of his death in 1984, the "great Egyptologist" Dee Jay Nelson was cooking hamburgers in a fast-food restaurant.

⁸⁵ For an explanation about various accounts of the First Vision, see page 40. For more about the film *The God Makers*, see page 67.

⁸⁶ See Lawrence Foster, "Career Apostates: Reflections on the Works of Jerald and Sandra Tanner," *Dialogue: A Journal of Mormon Thought* 17 (Summer 1984): 51. The "critic" mentioned published *Jerald and Sandra Tanner's Distorted View of Mormonism: A Response to* Mormonism—Shadow or Reality? anonymously as an "LDS Historian" in 1977.

⁸⁷ Foster, "Career Apostates," 45–46, 49.

⁸⁸ Bruce R. McConkie, *The Mortal Messiah: From Bethlehem to Calvary* (Salt Lake City, Utah: Deseret Book, 1981), 4:90.

Suggested Reading List

The following is a list of books about The Church of Jesus Christ of Latter-day Saints that give clear, unadulterated information about Church doctrine and programs. Included are several books which deal with anti-Mormon claims and confusion. Most of these books are available through LDS book stores or directly from the publisher. In addition, anyone who is interested in ongoing comment related to the LDS Church, and particularly Book of Mormon studies, should contact The Foundation for Ancient Research and Mormon Studies (FARMS), located in Provo, Utah (1-800-327-6715).

Ballard, M. Russell. *Our Search for Happiness.* Salt Lake City, Utah: Deseret Book, 1993.

Brown, Robert L., and Rosemary Brown. *They Lie in Wait to Deceive: A Study of Anti-Mormon Deception.* Mesa, Arizona: Brownsworth Publishing, vol. 1, 1981; vol. 2, 1984; vol. 3, 1986; vol. 4, 1995.

Bushman, Richard L. *Joseph Smith and the Beginnings of Mormonism.* Urbana: University of Illinois Press, 1984.

The Church of Jesus Christ of Latter-day Saints. *A Sure Foundation.* Salt Lake City, Utah: Deseret Book, 1988.

Embry, Jessie L. *Mormon Polygamous Families: Life in The Principle.* Salt Lake City: University of Utah Press, 1987.

Lee, Rex E. *What Do Mormons Believe?* Salt Lake City, Utah: Deseret Book, 1992.

Ludlow, Daniel H. *Encyclopedia of Mormonism.* New York: Macmillan, 1992.

Ludlow, Victor L. *Principles and Practices of the Restored Gospel.* Salt Lake City, Utah: Deseret Book, 1992.

McConkie, Bruce R. *Mormon Doctrine.* Salt Lake City, Utah: Bookcraft, 1979.

Nibley, Hugh W. *Tinkling Cymbals and Sounding Brass.* Salt Lake City, Utah: Deseret Book and FARMS, 1991.

————. *Since Cumorah.* Salt Lake City, Utah: Deseret Book and FARMS, 1967.

————. *Lehi in the Desert/The World of the Jaredites/There Were Jaredites.* Salt Lake City, Utah: Deseret Book and FARMS, 1988.

————. *The Prophetic Book of Mormon.* Salt Lake City, Utah: Deseret Book and FARMS, 1989.

Peterson, Daniel C., and Stephen D. Ricks. *Offenders for a Word.* Salt Lake City, Utah: Aspen Books, 1992.

Roberts, B. H. *A Comprehensive History of the Church.* Provo, Utah: Brigham Young University Press, 1965.

Robinson, Stephen E. *Are Mormons Christians?* Salt Lake City, Utah: Bookcraft, 1991.

Scharffs, Gilbert W. *The Truth About "The God Makers."* Salt Lake City, Utah: Publishers Press, 1989.

Van Wagoner, Richard S. *Mormon Polygamy: A History.* Salt Lake City, Utah: Signature Books, 1986.

Watt, George D. *Journal of Discourses.* 26 vols. Liverpool, England, 1855.

Widtsoe, John A. *Evidences and Reconciliations.* Salt Lake City, Utah: Bookcraft, 1987.